T0146948

EMANCIPATION(S)

RADICAL THINKERS }Ⅴ

"A golden treasury of theory" Eric Banks, *Bookforum*

"Beautifully designed...a sophisticated blend of theory and thought" Ziauddin Sardar, *New Statesman*

SET 1 ($12/£6/$14CAN)

MINIMA MORALIA
Reflections on a Damaged Life
THEODOR ADORNO
ISBN-13: 978 1 84467 051 2

FOR MARX
LOUIS ALTHUSSER
ISBN-13: 978 1 84467 052 9

THE SYSTEM OF OBJECTS
JEAN BAUDRILLARD
ISBN-13: 978 1 84467 053 6

LIBERALISM AND DEMOCRACY
NORBERTO BOBBIO
ISBN-13: 978 1 84467 062 8

THE POLITICS OF FRIENDSHIP
JACQUES DERRIDA
ISBN-13: 978 1 84467 054 3

THE FUNCTION OF CRITICISM
TERRY EAGLETON
ISBN-13: 978 1 84467 055 0

SIGNS TAKEN FOR WONDERS
On the Sociology of Literary Forms
FRANCO MORETTI
ISBN-13: 978 1 84467 056 7

THE RETURN OF THE POLITICAL
CHANTAL MOUFFE
ISBN-13: 978 1 84467 057 4

SEXUALITY IN THE FIELD OF VISION
JACQUELINE ROSE
ISBN-13: 978 1 84467 058 1

THE INFORMATION BOMB
PAUL VIRILIO
ISBN-13: 978 1 84467 059 8

CULTURE AND MATERIALISM
RAYMOND WILLIAMS
ISBN-13: 978 1 84467 060 4

THE METASTASES OF ENJOYMENT
On Women and Causality
SLAVOJ ŽIŽEK
ISBN-13: 978 1 84467 061 1

SET 2 ($12.95/£6.99/$17CAN)

AESTHETICS AND POLITICS
THEODOR ADORNO, WALTER BENJAMIN, ERNST BLOCH, BERTOLT BRECHT, GEORG LUKÁCS
ISBN-13: 978 1 84467 570 8

INFANCY AND HISTORY
On the Destruction of Experience
GIORGIO AGAMBEN
ISBN-13: 978 1 84467 571 5

POLITICS AND HISTORY
Montesquieu, Rousseau, Marx
LOUIS ALTHUSSER
ISBN-13: 978 1 84467 572 2

FRAGMENTS
JEAN BAUDRILLARD
ISBN-13: 978 1 84467 573 9

LOGICS OF DISINTEGRATION
Poststructuralist Thought and the Claims of Critical Theory
PETER DEWS
ISBN-13: 978 1 84467 574 6

LATE MARXISM
Adorno, Or, The Persistence of the Dialectic
FREDRIC JAMESON
ISBN-13: 978 1 84467 575 3

EMANCIPATION(S)
ERNESTO LACLAU
ISBN-13: 978 1 84467 576 0

THE POLITICAL DESCARTES
Reason, Ideology and the Bourgeois Project
ANTONIO NEGRI
ISBN-13: 978 1 84467 582 1

ON THE SHORES OF POLITICS
JACQUES RANCIÈRE
ISBN-13: 978 1 84467 577 7

STRATEGY OF DECEPTION
PAUL VIRILIO
ISBN-13: 978 1 84467 578 4

POLITICS OF MODERNISM
Against the New Conformists
RAYMOND WILLIAMS
ISBN-13: 978 1 84467 580 7

THE INDIVISIBLE REMAINDER
On Schelling and Related Matters
SLAVOJ ŽIŽEK
ISBN-13: 978 1 84467 581 4

First published by Verso 1996
© Ernesto Laclau 1996
This edition published by Verso 2007
All rights reserved

3 5 7 9 10 8 6 4 2

Verso
UK: 6 Meard Street, London W1F 0EG
USA: 20 Jay Street, Suite 1010, Brooklyn, NY 11201
www.versobooks.com

Verso is the imprint of New Left Books

ISBN-13: 978-1-84467-576-0
ISBN-10: 1-84467-576-9

British Library Cataloguing in Publication Data
A catalogue record for this book is available from the British Library

Library of Congress Cataloging-in-Publication Data
A catalog record for this book is available from the Library of Congress

Printed in the US

Contents

Preface

With the exception of the last piece in this volume, which was written in 1989, all the essays were written and published between 1991 and 1995. This period witnessed momentous changes in the world scene: the restructuring of the world order as a result of the collapse of the Eastern bloc; the civil war in former Yugoslavia; the growth of a populist right in Western Europe, whose racist politics were focused on its opposition to immigrants from Southern Europe and Northern Africa; the expansion of multicultural protest in North America; the end of apartheid in South Africa.

If we wanted briefly to characterize the distinctive features of the first half of the 1990s, I would say that they are to be found in the rebellion of various particularisms – ethnic, racial, national and sexual – against the totalizing ideologies which dominated the horizon of politics in the preceding decades. We could say that, in some way, the Cold War was – in the ideologies of its two protagonists – the last manifestation of the Enlightenment: that is, that we were dealing with ideologies which distributed the ensemble of the forces operating in the historical arena in two opposite camps, and which identified their own aims with those of a global human emancipation. Both 'free world' and 'communist society' were conceived by their defenders as projects of societies without internal frontiers or divisions.

It is the 'globality' of these projects that is in crisis. Whatever the sign of the new vision of politics which is emerging is going to be, it is clear that one of its basic dimensions is going to be the redefinition of the existing relation between universality and particularity. How is the unity – as relative as one wants – of the community to be viewed, when any approach to it must start from social and cultural particularisms not only stronger than in the past but constituting also the element defining the central imaginary of a group? Does not this imaginary exclude any identification with more universal human values? And, seen from the other angle, does not the very proliferation of antagonisms, the fact itself that there is not exact overlapping between cultural group and global community, require a language of 'rights' which must include the universalist reference that is in question?

These essays were written in the conviction that both universalism and particularism are two ineradicable dimensions in the making of political identities, but that the articulation between them is far from being evident. Some of the essays briefly summarize the most important historical stages in the thinking of this articulation. We could say, with reference to the contemporary scene, that the dominant tendencies have been polarized around two positions. One of them unilaterally privileges universalism and sees in a dialogical process a way of reaching a consensus transcending all particularism (Habermas); the other, dedicated to the celebration of pure particularism and contextualism, proclaims the death of the universal (as in some forms of postmodernism). For reasons that are presented *in extenso* in the essays, neither of these extreme positions is acceptable to me. But what is important to determine is the logic of a possible mediation between the two. The main thesis of these essays is that such a mediation can only be a hegemonic one (which involves reference to the universal as an empty place), and that the operation it performs modifies the identities of both the particular and the universal. It is for the reader to judge what is achieved through this kind of approach.

A last word about the occasions on which these essays were written. In all cases they were circumstantial interventions, taking place around a concrete event. They should be seen as provisional explorations rather than as fully-fledged theoretical constructs, as answers to the ethical and political imperative of intervening in debates about transformations which were taking place before our eyes. Thus their *ad hoc* character, their inevitable repetitions, and their lacunae. I hope, anyway, that they can be useful in throwing a certain light on some of the more pressing political problems of our time.

Princeton, October 1995

Acknowledgements

'Beyond Emancipation' was originally presented as a paper at a conference held at the Institute of Social Studies, The Hague, 30–31 January 1991, and published in Jan Nederveen Pieterse (ed.), *Emancipations, Modern and Postmodern*, London, Sage 1992.

'Universalism, Particularism and the Question of Identity' was originally delivered at a symposium held on 16–17 November 1991 at City University, New York. It was published in John Rajchman (ed.), *The Identity in Question*, New York and London, Routledge 1995.

'Why do Empty Signifiers Matter to Politics?' was published in Jeffrey Weeks (ed.), *The Lesser Evil and the Greater Good. The Theory and Politics of Social Diversity*, London, Rivers Oram Press 1994.

'Subject of Politics, Politics of the Subject' was delivered at the Seventh East-West Philosophers Conference on 'Democracy and Justice: A Philosophical Exploration', held in Honolulu on 9–23 January 1995 and sponsored by the Department of Philosophy, University of Hawaii, in co-operation with the East-West Centre. It was published in *Differences*, 7.1, Spring 1995.

'The Time is Out of Joint' was delivered in Leeds on 9 September 1995, as the keynote speech of a conference on 'Ghosts', organized by the Centre for Critical and Cultural Theory, University of Wales, Cardiff, and the University of Leeds. It was published in *Diacritics*, vol. 25, no. 2, Summer 1995.

'Power and Representation' was originally delivered at the Critical Theory Institute, University of California, Irvine in 1989. The present is an expanded version published in Mark Poster (ed.), *Politics, Theory and Contemporary Culture*, New York, Columbia University Press 1993.

'Community and its Paradoxes: Richard Rorty's "Liberal Utopia"' was originally published in Miami Theory Collective (ed.), *Community at Loose Ends*, Minnesota University Press 1991.

1

Beyond Emancipation

I see 'emancipation' – a notion which has been part of our political imaginary for centuries and whose disintegration we are witnessing today – as being organized around six distinctive dimensions. The first is what we could call the *dichotomic dimension*: between the emancipatory moment and the social order which has preceded it there is an absolute chasm, a radical discontinuity. The second can be considered a *holistic dimension*: emancipation affects all areas of social life and there is a relation of essential imbrication between its various contents in these different areas. The third dimension can be referred to as the *transparency dimension*: if alienation in its various aspects – religious, political, economic, etcetera – has been radically eradicated, there is only the absolute coincidence of human essence with itself and there is no room for any relation of either power or representation. Emancipation presupposes the elimination of power, the abolition of the subject/object distinction, and the management – without any opaqueness or mediation – of communitarian affairs by social agents identified with the viewpoint of social totality. It is in this sense that in Marxism, for instance, communism and the withering away of the state logically entail each other. A fourth dimension is the *pre-existence* of what has to be emancipated *vis-à-vis* the act of emancipation. There is no emancipation without oppression, and there is no oppression without the presence of something which is impeded in its free development by oppressive forces. Emancipation is not, in this sense, an act of *creation* but instead of liberation of something which precedes the liberating act. In the fifth place, we can speak of a *dimension of ground* which is inherent in the project of any radical emancipation. If the act of emancipation is truly radical, if it is really going to leave behind everything preceding it, it has to take place at the level of the 'ground' of the social. If there is no ground, if the revolutionary act leaves a residue which is beyond the transforming abilities of the emancipatory praxis, the very idea of a *radical* emancipation would become contradictory. Finally, we can speak of a *rationalistic dimension*. This is the point where the emancipatory discourses of secularized eschatologies part company with the religious ones. For religious eschatologies the absorption of the real within a total system of representation does not require the rationality of the latter: it is enough that the inscrutable designs of God are transmitted to us through revelation. But in a secular eschatology this is not possible. As the idea of an absolute representability of the real cannot appeal to anything external to the real itself, it can only coincide with the principle of an absolute rationality. Thus, full emancipation is simply the moment in which the real ceases to be an opaque positivity confronting us, and in which the latter's distance from the rational is finally cancelled.

To what extent do these six dimensions conform to a logically unified whole? Do they constitute a coherent theoretical structure? I shall try to show that they do not, and that the assertion of the classical notion of emancipation in its many variants has involved the advancement of incompatible logical claims. This should not lead us, however, to the simple abandonment of the logic of emancipation. It is, on the contrary, by playing within the system of logical incompatibilities of the latter that we can open the way to new liberating discourses which are no longer hindered by the antinomies and blind alleys to which the classical notion of emancipation has led.

Let us start with the dichotomic dimension. The dichotomy that we are facing here is of a very particular kind. It is not a simple *difference* between two elements or stages which contemporarily or successively coexist with each other, and which in that way contribute to the constitution of each other's differential identity. If we are speaking about *real* emancipation, the 'other' opposing the emancipated identity cannot be a purely positive or neutral other but, instead, an 'other' which prevents the full constitution of the identity of the first element. In that sense, the dichotomy involved in the emancipatory act is in a relation of logical solidarity with our fourth dimension – the pre-existence of the identity to be emancipated *vis-à-vis* the act of emancipation. It is easy to see why: without this pre-existence there would be no identity to repress or prevent from fully developing, and the very notion of emancipation would become meaningless. Now, an unavoidable conclusion follows from this: *true* emancipation requires a *real* 'other' – that is, an 'other' who cannot be reduced to any of the figures of the 'same'. But, in that case, between the identity to be emancipated and the 'other' opposing it, there can be no positive objectivity underlying and constituting the identity of both poles of the dichotomy.

A very simple consideration can help to clarify this point. Let us suppose for a moment that there is a deeper objective process giving its meaning to both sides of the dichotomy. If so, the chasm constituting the dichotomy loses its radical character. If the dichotomy is not constitutive but is rather the *expression* of a positive process, the 'other' cannot be a *real* other: given that the dichotomy is grounded in an objective necessity, the oppositional dimension is also necessary and, in that sense, it is part of the identity of the two forces confronting each other. The perception of the other as a radical other can only be a matter of appearance. If a stone is broken when it clashes with another stone, it would be absurd to say that the second stone negates the identity of the first – on the contrary, being broken in certain circumstances expresses the identity of the stone as much as remaining unaltered if the circumstances are different. The characteristic of an objective process is that it reduces to its own logic the totality of its constitutive moments. The 'other' can only be the result of an internal differentiation of the 'same' and, as a result, it is entirely subordinated to the latter. But this is not the otherness that the chasm of the emancipatory act requires. There would be no break, no true emancipation if the act constitutive of the latter was only the result of the internal differentiation of the oppressing system.

This can be expressed in an only slightly different way by saying that if the emancipation is a true one, it will be incompatible with any kind of 'objective' explanation. I can certainly explain a set of circumstances that *made possible* the emergence of an oppressive system. I can explain *how* forces antagonistic to that system were constituted and evolved. But the strict moment of the confrontation between both of them, *if the chasm is a radical one*, will be refractory to any kind of objective explanation. Between two incompatible discourses, each of them constituting the pole of an antagonism between them, there is no common measure, and the strict moment of the clash between them cannot be explained in objective terms. Unless, of course, the antagonistic moment is purely a matter of appearance and the conflict between social forces is assimilated to a natural process, as in the clash between the two stones. But, as we said, this is incompatible with the otherness required by the founding act of emancipation.

Now, if the dichotomic dimension requires the radical otherness of a past which has to be thrown away, in that case, this dimension is incompatible with most of the others which we have presented as constitutive of the classical notion of emancipation. In the first place, dichotomic radicalism and radical ground are incompatible. As we have seen, the condition of the radical chasm that the emancipatory logic requires is the irreducible otherness of the oppressive system which is rejected. But, in that case, there can be no single ground explaining *both* the order which is rejected and the order that emancipation inaugurates. The alternative is clear: *either* emancipation is radical and, in that case, it has to be its own ground and confine what it excludes to a radical otherness constituted by evil or irrationality; *or* there is a deeper ground which establishes the rational connections between the pre-emancipatory order, the new 'emancipated' one and the transition between both – in which case, emancipation cannot be considered as a truly *radical* foundation. The philosophers of the Enlightenment were perfectly consequent when they asserted that if a rational society was a fully-fledged order resulting from a radical break with the past, any organization previous to that break could only be conceived as the product of ignorance and of the folly of men, that is as deprived of any rationality. The difficulty, however, is that if the founding act of a truly rational society is conceived as the victory over the irrational forces of the past – forces which have no common measure with the victorious new social order – the founding act itself cannot be rational but is itself utterly contingent and depends on a relation of power. In that case, the emancipated social order also becomes purely contingent and cannot be considered as the liberation of any true human essence. We are in the same dilemma as before: if we want to assert the rationality and permanence of the new social order that we are establishing, we have to extend that rationality to the founding act itself and, as a result, to the social order which is to be overthrown – but in that case, the radicalism of the dichotomic dimension vanishes. If, on the contrary, we assert this latter radicalism, both the founding act and the social order resulting from it become entirely contingent; that is, the conditions for a permanent structural outside have been created and what now vanishes is the dimension of ground in the classical notion of emancipation.

This incompatibility within the discourse of emancipation between the dichotomic dimension and the dimension of ground creates two fundamental matrices around which all the other dimensions are organized. As we have said, the pre-existence of the oppressed *vis-à-vis* the oppressing force is a corollary of the radicalism of the chasm required by the dichotomic dimension; if the oppressed did not pre-exist the oppressing order, it would be an effect of the latter and, in that case, the chasm would be constitutive. (A different matter is whether the chasm is not represented by the oppressed through forms of identification which *presuppose* the presence of the oppressor. We shall return later to this point.) But all the other dimensions logically require the presence of a positive ground and are, consequently, incompatible with the constitutivity of the chasm required by the dichotomic dimension. Holism would be impossible unless a positive ground of the social unifies in a self-contained totality the variety of its partial processes, antagonisms and dichotomies included. But in that case, the chasm has to be internal to the social order and not a dividing line separating social order from something outside it. Transparency requires full representability, and there is no possibility of achieving it if the opaqueness inherent in radical otherness is constitutive of social relations. Finally, as we have seen, in secularized eschatologies full representability is equivalent to full knowledge – understood as full reduction of the real to the rational – and this is only achievable if the other is reduced to the same.

So, we can see that the discourses of emancipation have been historically constituted through the putting together of two incompatible lines of thought: one that presupposes the objectivity and full representability of the social, the other whose whole case depends on showing that there is a chasm which makes any social objectivity ultimately impossible. Now, the important point is that these two opposite lines of thought are not simple analytical mistakes so that we could choose between one or the other and formulate an emancipatory discourse which would be free of logical inconsistencies. The matter is more complicated than that because these two lines of thought are equally necessary for the production of an emancipatory discourse. It is by asserting both of them that the notion of emancipation becomes meaningful. Emancipation means *at one and the same time* radical foundation and radical exclusion; that is, it postulates, at the same time, both a ground of the social and its impossibility. It is necessary that an emancipated society is fully transparent to itself and at the same time that this transparency is constituted through its demarcation from essential opaqueness, with the result that the demarcating line cannot be thought from the side of transparency and that transparency itself becomes opaque. It is necessary that a rational society is a self-enclosed totality which subordinates to itself all its partial processes; but the limits of this holistic configuration – without which there would be no holistic configuration at all – can only be established by differentiating the latter from an exterior which is irrational and formless. We have to conclude that the two lines of thought are logically incompatible and yet require each other: without them the whole notion of emancipation would crumble.

What follows, however, from this logical incompatibility? In what way does the notion of emancipation crumble as its result? It is clear that it only crumbles in a *logical* terrain, but it does not follow at all that this is enough to make it non-operative *socially* – unless, of course, we espouse the absurd hypothesis that the social terrain is structured as a logical one and that contradictory propositions cannot have social effectivity. We must carefully distinguish two very different assertions at this point. The first is that the principle of contradiction does not apply to society and that, as a result, somebody can be and not be in the same place at the same time, or that the same piece of legislation has been both promulgated and not promulgated, etcetera. I do not think that anybody would be bold enough to formulate this kind of proposition. But it is a completely different proposition to assert that social practices construct concepts and institutions whose inner logic is based on the operation of incompatible logics. And, obviously, here there is no denial of the principle of contradiction, because to say the opposite would be to assert that it is logically contradictory to formulate contradictory propositions, which certainly is not the case. Now, if the operation of contradictory logics can perfectly well be at the root of many institutions and social practices, a problem arises as to the extent to which this operation is possible. Could it be the case that incompatible logics operate within society but cannot be extended to society as a whole; that is, that formulating contradictory propositions in certain circumstances is a logical requirement for society as a whole not to be contradictory? Here we are close to Hegel's 'cunning of reason'. But it is clear that in this case we are dealing with an *ontological* hypothesis, not with a *logical* requirement. And this ontological hypothesis is nothing other than a new formulation of the 'dimension of ground' that we have already discussed.

But what about the hypothesis itself? Is it logically impeccable and our only task to determine if it is right or wrong? Evidently not, because everything that we have said about the logic of the ground and its concomitant dimensions – transparency, holism, etcetera fully applies here. Transparency, as we have seen, constitutes itself as a terrain through the act of excluding opaqueness. But what about the act of exclusion itself, what about the constitutive *difference* between transparency and opaqueness: is it transparent or opaque? It is clear that the alternative is undecidable, and that the two equally possible logical moves – to make the opaque transparent or to make the transparent opaque – blur the neatness of the alternative.

This whole digression on the status of logical contradictions in society is important to make us aware of two aspects which have to be taken into account in dealing with the language games that it is possible to play within the logic of emancipation. The first is that if the term 'emancipation' is to remain meaningful, it is impossible to renounce either of its two incompatible sides. Rather, we have to play one against the other in ways which have to be specified. The second aspect is that this double and contradictory requirement is not simply something that we have to assert *if* emancipation is to be maintained as a relevant political term. If that was the whole problem, we could avoid it just by denying that emancipation is a valid concept and by asserting the validity of either of the two logics taken separately. But this is precisely what is not possible: our analysis has led us to the conclusion that it is the contradictory sides themselves that require the presence and, at the same time, the exclusion of each other: each is both the condition of possibility and the condition of impossibility of the other. Thus, we are not simply dealing with a logical incompatibility but rather with a real *undecidability* between the two sides. This already indicates to us the way in which the logic of emancipation has to be approached: by looking at the effects which follow from the subversion of each of its two incompatible sides by the other. The very possibility of this analysis results from what we said earlier: the social operation of two incompatible logics does not consist in a pure and simple annulment of their respective effects but in a specific set of mutual deformations. This is precisely what we understand by subversion. It is as if each of the two incompatible logics presupposes a full operation that the other is denying, and that this denial leads to an orderly set of subversive effects of the internal structure of both of them. It is clear that in analysing these subversive effects we are not witnessing the rise of something new that leaves both logics behind but, rather, an orderly drifting away from what would otherwise have been their full operation.

Before we move on to describe the general pattern of this drifting away, however, we have to consider the way in which classical emancipatory discourses dealt with our basically incompatible dimensions, which certainly did not go entirely unnoticed. A discourse of radical emancipation emerged for the first time with Christianity, and its specific form was *salvation*. With elements partly inherited from Jewish apocalypse, Christianity was going to present the image of a future humanity – or post-humanity – from which all evil would have been eradicated. Both the dichotomic and the ground dimensions are present here: world history is a permanent struggle between the saints and the forces of evil, and there is no common ground between them; the future society will be a perfect one without any internal splits, opaqueness or alienation; the various alternatives in the struggle against the forces of evil and the final triumph of God are known to us by revelation. Now, within this world-embracing picture, we see the emergence of a theological difficulty which is nothing but the theological recognition of our two incompatible dimensions. God is almighty and absolute goodness, the creator *ex nihilo* of everything existing and the absolute source and ground of all created beings. In that case, how do we explain the presence of evil in the world? The alternative is clear: either God is almighty and the source of everything existing – and, in that case, He cannot be absolute goodness because He is responsible for the presence of evil in the world – or He is not responsible for such a presence and, therefore, is not almighty. We see emerging here the same problem that we posed in non-theological terms: either the dichotomy separating good and evil is a radical one, without common ground between the two poles; or there is such a ground and, in that case, the radicalism of the opposition between good and evil is blurred. Christian thought, confronted with this alternative, oscillated between asserting that the designs of God are inscrutable and that the dilemma was the result of the limitation of human reason – so that the problem was set aside without solution – and looking for a solution which, if it was going to be consistent at all, could only maintain an image of God as absolute source by asserting in one way or another the necessary character of evil. Eriugena, asserting in the Carolingian renaissance that God reaches perfection through necessary phases of transition involving finitude, contingency and evil, started a tradition which, passing through Northern mysticism, Nicholas Cusanus and Spinoza, would reach its highest point in Hegel and Marx.

The Christian vision of history was also confronted with another problem – this time without contradiction – and that is the incommensurability existing between the universality of the tasks to be performed and the limitations of the finite agents in charge of them. The category of incarnation was designed in order to mediate between these two incommensurable realities. The paradigm of all incarnation is, of course, the advent of Christ himself, but each of the universal moments in world history is marked by divine interventions through which finite bodies have to take up universal tasks which were not predetermined in the least by their concrete finitude. The dialectic of incarnation presupposes the infinite distance between the incarnating body and the incarnated task. It is only God's mediation that establishes a bridge between the two, for motives which escape human reason. Returning to our various dimensions of emancipation, we can say that in Christian discourse transparency is ensured at the level of *representation* but not at the level of *knowledge*. Revelation gives us a representation of the totality of history, but the rationality which expresses itself in that story will always escape us. That is why the rationalistic dimension had to be absent from theological accounts of salvation.

It is this chasm between representation and rationality that modern eschatologies will attempt to bridge. Since God is no longer in the foreground as guarantor of total representability, the ground has to show its all-embracing abilities without any appeal to an infinite distance from what it actually embraces. So total representation becomes possible only as total rationality. The first consequence of this modern trend is that the turn insinuated in pantheistic and semi-pantheistic versions of Christianity is brought now to its logical conclusions. If there is a ground out of which human history shows itself as purely rational – and, as a result, fully transparent to itself – evil, opaqueness, otherness can only be the result of partial and distorted representations. The more the dimension of ground imposes itself, the more the irretrievable alterity of the chasm inherent in the dichotomic dimension has to be dismissed as false consciousness. We have mentioned before the Hegelian 'cunning of reason'. But the Marxian versions of the same principle are not far away. It is enough to remember the description of the emergence and development of antagonistic societies: primitive communism had to disintegrate in order to develop the productive forces of humanity; the latter's development required, as its historical and logical condition, the passage through the hell of the successive exploitative regimes; and it is only at the end of the process, when history reaches the peak of a new communism representing a further development of the productive forces, that the meaning and rationality of all the previous suffering is finally shown. As Hegel said, universal history is not the terrain of happiness. Seen from the vantage point of universal history, everything – slavery, obscurantism, terrorism, exploitation, Auschwitz – reveals its rational substance. Radical rejection, antagonism, ethical incompatibilities, in sum anything linked to the dichotomic dimension, belong to the realm of superstructures, to the way in which social actors live (distortedly) their relations to their real conditions. As it was asserted in a famous text:

> The changes in the economic foundation lead sooner or later to the transformation of the whole immense superstructure. In studying such transformations it is always necessary to distinguish between the material transformation of the economic conditions of production, which

can be distinguished with the precision of natural science, and the legal, political, religious, artistic or philosophic – in short, ideological forms in which men become conscious of this conflict and fight it out. Just as one does not judge an individual by what he thinks about himself, so one cannot judge such a period of transformation by its consciousness, but, on the contrary, this consciousness must be explained from the contradictions of material life, from the conflict existing between the social forces of production and the relations of production.[1]

So, in this reading the dichotomic dimension becomes a 'superstructure' of the dimension of ground, and emancipation becomes a mere rhetorical ornament of a substantive process which has to be understood in entirely different terms. As a result of that, the second logical requirement of this essential turn is that we have to do away altogether with the dialectic of incarnation. As we have seen, incarnation requires connection between two elements through the mediation of a third external to them, in such a way that, left to themselves, there is an unbridgeable distance between the first two elements: without the third element there would be no connection at all between them. So incarnation was possible as long as God was part of the *explanans*, but if He retreats to the background, the connection between incarnated universality and incarnating body becomes impossible. That is, a fully rationalistic and secular eschatology has to show the possibility of a universal actor who is beyond the contradictions between particularity and universality, or rather, one whose particularity expresses in a direct way, without any system of mediations, pure and universal human essence. This actor is for Marx the proletariat, whose particularity expresses universality in such a direct fashion that his advent is conceived as the end of the need for any process of representation. No incarnation can take place here. But if we look at the matter closely, we shall see that this actor, who is presented as the only one who can carry out a true process of emancipation, is precisely the one for whom 'emancipation' has become a meaningless term. How do we construct the identity of this actor? As we have seen, the agent of emancipation has to be one whose identity is prevented in its constitution/development by an existing oppressive regime. But if the process of disintegration of that regime and the process of formation of the 'emancipatory' actor are the same, then we can hardly say that s/he is oppressed by the same regime that constitutes him or her.

11

We can, of course, perfectly well argue that the proletariat is the product of capitalist development, for only the latter creates the separation between the direct producer and the ownership of the means of production, but this only explains the emergence of the proletariat as a particular subject position within capitalist society, not the emergence of the proletariat as an emancipatory subject. In order to have the latter, we need to show that the capitalist negates in the worker something which is not the mere product of capitalism. In our terminology: we need to show that there is an antagonistic dichotomy which is not reducible to a single ground. That is, that the condition of true emancipation is, as we have mentioned before, a constitutive opaqueness that no grounding can eradicate. This means that the two operations of closure which founded the political discourse of modernity have to be unmade. If, on the one hand, modernity started by strictly tying representability to knowledge, the constitutive opaqueness resulting from the dialectic of emancipation involves not only that society is no longer transparent to knowledge, but also – since God is no longer there to substitute knowledge by revelation – that all representation will be necessarily partial and will take place against the background of an essential unrepresentability. On the other hand, this constitutive opaqueness withdraws the ground which had made it possible to go beyond the dialectic of incarnation, given that there is no longer a transparent society in which the universal can show itself in a direct unmediated way. But again, as God is no longer there, ensuring through His word the knowledge of a universal destiny which escapes human reason, opaqueness cannot lead to a restoration of the dialectic of incarnation either. The death of the ground seems to lead to the death of the universal and to the dissolution of social struggles into mere particularism. This is the other dimension of the emancipatory logic that we stressed before: if the absence of a ground is the condition of radical emancipation, the radicalism of the founding emancipatory act cannot be conceived otherwise but as an act of grounding.

So it looks as if whatever direction we take, emancipation becomes impossible. However, we hesitate to extend a death certificate. For, although we have explored the logical cons-equences which follow from each of the two alternatives taken separately, we have still said nothing about the effects that could derive from the social interaction of these two symmetrical impossibilities. Let us consider the matter carefully. Emancipation is strictly linked to the destiny of the universal. If the dimension of ground is going to prevail, or if emancipation is going to be a true act of radical foundation, its performance cannot be the work of any particularistic social agency. We have seen that these two dimensions – ground and radical chasm – are actually incompatible, but both alternatives equally require the presence of the universal. Without the emergence of the universal within the historical terrain, emancipation becomes impossible. In theological thought, as we have seen, this presence of the universal was guaranteed by the logic of incarnation, which mediated between particularistic finitude and universal task. In secularized eschatologies, the universal had to emerge without any kind of mediation: the 'universal class' in Marx can perform its emancipatory job because it has become, precisely, pure human essence which has abandoned any particularistic belonging. Now, the ultimate logical impossibility of either a chasm which is truly radical, or of the dissolution of emancipation in some version of the 'cunning of reason', seems to destroy the very possibility of any totalizing effects. With this the only terrain in which the universal could emerge – that is social totality – has apparently disappeared. Does this mean that this death of the universal, with the impossibility of emancipation as its necessary corollary, leaves us in a purely particularistic world in which social actors pursue only limited objectives? One moment of reflection is enough to show us that this is not an adequate conclusion. 'Particularism' is an essentially relational concept: something is particular in relation to other particularities and the ensemble of them presupposes a social totality within which they are constituted. So, if it is the very notion of a social totality that is in question, the notion of 'particular' identities is equally threatened. The category of totality continues haunting us through the effects that derive from its very absence.

This last remark opens the way to a form of conceiving the relationship between universalism and particularism which differs from both an incarnation of one in the other and the cancellation of their difference and which, in fact, creates the possibility of new discourses of liberation. These go, certainly, beyond emancipation, but are constructed by movements taking place within the system of alternatives generated by the latter. Let us start our analysis with the consideration of any social antagonism

– for instance, a national minority which is oppressed by an authoritarian state. There is a chasm here between the two, and we already know that there is in all chasms a basic undecidability as to which of its two sides the line separating them belongs. Let us suppose that at some point other antagonistic forces – a foreign invasion, the action of hostile economic forces, etcetera – intervene. The national minority will see all the antagonistic forces as *equivalent* threats to its own identity. Now, if there is equivalence, this means that through all the very different antagonistic forces something equally present in all of them is expressed. This common element, however, cannot be something positive because, from the point of view of their concrete positive features, each of these forces differs from the other. So it has to be something purely negative: the threat that each of them poses to the national identity. The conclusion is that in a relation of equivalence, each of the equivalent elements functions as a symbol of negativity as such, of a certain universal impossibility which penetrates the identity in question. To put the matter in other terms: in an antagonistic relation, that which operates as a negative pole of a certain identity is constitutively split. All its contents express a general negativity transcending them. But for that reason, the 'positive' pole cannot be reduced to its concrete contents either: if that which opposes them is the universal form of negativity as such, these contents have to express, through their equivalential relation, the universal form of fullness or identity. We are not dealing here with 'determinate negation' in the Hegelian sense: while the latter comes out of the apparent positivity of the concrete and 'circulates' through contents that are always determinate, our notion of negativity depends on the failure in the constitution of all determination.

This constitutive split shows the emergence of the universal within the particular. But it shows as well that the relation between particularity and universality is an essentially unstable and undecidable one. What particular content was going to incarnate universality was God's decision in Christian eschatologies and was, as a result, entirely fixed and predetermined. As self-transparent universality was a moment in the rational self-development of particularity, which particular actor was going to abolish his or her distance from the universal, was something equally fixed by essential determinations in the Hegelian/Marxist vision of history. But if the universal results from a constitutive split in which the negation of a particular identity transforms this identity in the symbol of identity and fullness as such, in that case, we have to conclude that: (1) the universal has no content of its own, but is an absent fullness or, rather, the signifier of fullness as such, of the very idea of fullness; (2) the universal can only emerge out of the particular, because it is only the negation of a *particular* content that transforms that content in the symbol of a universality transcending it; (3) since, however, the universal – taken by itself – is an empty signifier, *what* particular content is going to symbolize the latter is something which cannot be determined either by an analysis of the particular in itself or of the universal. The relation between the two depends on the context of the antagonism and it is, in the strict sense of the term, a hegemonic operation. It is as if the undecidable line separating the two poles of the dichotomy had expanded its undecidable effects to the interior of the poles themselves, to the very relation between universality and particularity.

Let us now consider, in the light of these conclusions, what happens to the six dimensions of the notion of emancipation with which we started. The dimension of ground, we have shown, is incompatible with emancipation and it also involves us in insurmountable logical aporias. Does this, however, mean that we can have no further dealings with the notion of 'ground', that it has to be merely abandoned? Obviously not, if for no other reason than because disaggregation and particularism, which constitute the only possible alternative, presuppose, at the same time that they deny, the notion of ground. It is possible, however, to make the interplay of these incompatible logics the very locus of a certain political productivity. Particularity both denies and requires totality, that is the ground. These contradictory movements express themselves in what we have called the constitutive split of all concrete identity. Totality is impossible and, at the same time, is required by the particular: in that sense, it is present in the particular as that which is absent, as a constitutive lack which constantly forces the particular to be more than itself, to assume a universal role which can only be precarious and unsutured. It is because of this that we can have democratic politics: a succession of finite and particular identities which attempt to assume universal tasks surpassing them; but that, as a result, are never able to entirely conceal the distance

15

between task and identity, and can always be substituted by alternative groups. Incompletion and provisionality belong to the essence of democracy.

It goes without saying that the holistic dimension moves along the same path as the dimension of ground: the two of them are, in fact, the same dimension seen from two different angles. As far as the rationalistic dimension is concerned, we should take into account that the secularist turn of modernity involved both the assertion that the meaning of history is not to be found outside history itself, that there is no supernatural power operating as the ultimate source of everything that exists, and the very different assertion that this purely worldly succession of events is an entirely rational process that human beings can intellectually master. Thus reason reoccupies the terrain that Christianity had attributed to God. But the eclipse of the ground deprives reason of its all-embracing abilities and only the first assertion (or rather commitment), the intraworldly character of all explanation, remains. Reason is necessary, but it is also impossible. The presence of its absence is shown in the various attempts to 'rationalize' the world that finite social agents carry out. Precariousness and ultimate failure (if we persist in measuring success by an old rationalistic standard) are certainly the destiny of these attempts, but through this failure we gain something perhaps more precious than the certainty that we are losing: a freedom *vis-à-vis* the different forms of identification, which are impotent to imprison us within the network of an unappealable logic. The same applies to the dimension of transparency: total representability is no longer there as a possibility, but this does not mean that its necessity has been eradicated. This unbridgeable gap between possibility and necessity leads straight into what Nietzsche called a 'war of interpretations'. If limited and finite beings try to know, to make the world transparent to themselves, it is impossible that this limitation and finitude is not transmitted to the products of their intellectual activity. In this sense, the abandonment of the aspiration to 'absolute' knowledge has exhilarating effects: on the one hand, human beings can recognize themselves as the true creators and no longer as the passive recipients of a predetermined structure; on the other hand, as all social agents have to recognize their concrete finitude, nobody can aspire to be the true consciousness of the world. This opens the way to an endless interaction between various perspectives and makes ever more distant the possibility of any totalitarian dream.

What about those aspects that are incompatible with the dimension of ground and the ones depending on it? As we have seen, the dichotomic dimension presupposes the structural location of a ground and, at the same time, makes the latter unthinkable. Only if it takes place at the level of a ground of the social is the chasm constituting the dichotomy radical from the point of view of its *location*, but the operation that the dichotomy performs – the *separation* of emancipation from a totally alien past – is logically incompatible with the notion of such a structural location. Now, as in the case of the other dimensions, some positive consequences follow from this double movement of self-positing and withdrawal of the ground. The most important one is that if, on the one hand, no dichotomy is absolute, there can be no act of fully revolutionary foundation; but if, on the other hand, this dichotomization is not the result of an elimination of radical otherness but, on the contrary, of the very impossibility of its total eradication, partial and precarious dichotomies have to be constitutive of the social fabric. This precariousness and incompletion of the frontiers constituting social division are at the root of the contemporary possibility of a general autonomization of social struggles – the so-called new social movements – instead of subordinating them to a unique frontier which would be the only source of social division. Finally, the *pre-existence* of the identity to be emancipated *vis-à-vis* the oppressive forces is also subverted and submitted to the same contradictory movement that the other dimensions experience. In classical discourses, the emancipated identities had to pre-exist the act of emancipation as a result of their radical otherness *vis-à-vis* the forces opposing them. It is true that this is unavoidable in any antagonistic struggle; but if, at the same time, dichotomization is not truly radical – and as we have just seen it cannot be so – then the identity of the oppressive forces has to be in some way inscribed in the identity searching for emancipation. This contradictory situation is expressed in the undecidability between internality and externality of the oppressor in relation to the oppressed: to be oppressed is part of my identity as a subject struggling for emancipation; without the presence of the oppressor my identity would be different.

17

The constitution of the latter requires and at the same time rejects the presence of the other.

Contemporary social struggles are bringing to the fore this contradictory movement that the emancipatory discourse of both religious and modern secularized eschatologies had concealed and repressed. We are today coming to terms with our own finitude and with the political possibilities that it opens. This is the point from which the potentially liberatory discourses of our postmodern age have to start. We can perhaps say that today we are at the end of emancipation and at the beginning of freedom.[2]

Notes

1. Karl Marx, *A Contribution to the Critique of Political Economy*, London, Lawrence and Wishart 1971, p. 24.

2. Since this essay was originally published in 1992, a considerable set of misunderstandings has arisen around its last sentence. Does asserting that we are at the beginning of freedom imply negating everything that the essay sustains? If freedom is self-determination, in what sense would that freedom be different from the one postulated by the classical notion of emancipation? It is necessary to dissipate this misunderstanding. By freedom I do not mean a positive and unnuanced fullness, but something essentially ambiguous. To make this point perfectly clear, I want to reproduce the last question (together with my answer) that David Howarth and Aletta Norval put to me in a recent interview for the journal *Angelaki* ('Negotiating the Paradoxes of Contemporary Politics. An Interview with Ernesto Laclau', *Angelaki*, Oxford, Angelaki 1994, 1:3, pp. 43–50).

D.H. and A.N: In your work the category of dislocation has taken on a more and more central role. This is so especially with regard to your claim that 'dislocation is the source of freedom'. A number of questions regarding the relation between dislocation and freedom, and the nature of freedom itself, arise here. It is with the nature of the movement from dislocation to 'freedom' that we are mainly concerned. How are we to understand the nature of this freedom? You distance yourself very clearly from accounts which emphasize the 'freedom of a subject with a positive identity' (*New Reflections on the Revolution of Our Time*, Verso 1990, p. 60), arguing that freedom here is that of a 'structural fault'. Thus, freedom has no positive contents but is 'mere possibility'. However, seen from the vantage point of dislocation, there is no freedom here. The failure of the structure fully to constitute the subject, forces the subject to be subject, to take a decision, to act, to identify anew. We have to respond, we are not free. It seems, therefore, that the relation of dislocation/freedom could be thought more productively, by emphasizing both the dimension of possibility and its impossibility. That is to say, rather than simply being free to act, to choose in a Sartrean sense, the moment of freedom and possibility is simultaneously the moment of my greatest constraint, of unfreedom. Taking this latter dimension into account could – to come back to our contemporary situation – help to make sense of the experience of dislocation as not being *ipso facto* something positive and worthy of celebration. In other words, would you agree that stressing the terror and force at the heart of freedom, has to form part of our very account of the possibilities arising out of severe dislocation?

E.L.: I could not agree more with your conclusion. As you cogently point out, the experience of dislocation is not *ipso facto* 'something positive and worthy of celebration'. But this also means that, if freedom and dislocation are related in the way I have suggested – that you seem to accept – the very experience of freedom is ambiguous. For that reason, although as I said, I subscribe to your conclusion, I cannot follow you in one of the intermediate stages of your argument, when you assert that, because the failure of the structure 'forces the subject to be a subject', when we are forced to respond we are unfree. If this was so, we would certainly be in the best of all possible worlds: the villain of the piece would be 'dislocation', while 'freedom', as complete lack of constraint, would be preserved as an uncontaminated positive value. But, as you yourself recognize, this impeccable solution is impossible: freedom and dislocation cannot be separated that way. On the one hand, a freedom that dislocation does not coerce to choose, would not be my freedom but the freedom of the structure which has constructed me as a subject. On the other hand, a freedom which is my freedom, which avoids both the pitfalls of the Spinozian freedom, reduced to consciousness of necessity, and the Sartrean freedom of being a chooser who has no longer any grounds to choose, can only be the freedom of a structural failure – i.e. dislocation. But in that case the ambiguity of dislocation (what you call 'the terror and force at the heart of freedom') contaminates freedom itself. Freedom is both liberating and enslaving, exhilarating and traumatic, enabling and destructive. In a fragmented and heterogeneous society, the spaces of freedom certainly increase, but this is not a phenomenon which is uniformly positive, because it also installs in those spaces the ambiguity of freedom. As a result, the possibility emerges of more radical attempts at renouncing freedom than those that we have known in the past. If freedom and dislocation go together, it is in the terrain of a generalized freedom that experiences such as those of contemporary totalitarianism become possible. If this is so, it means that the quest for an absolute freedom for the subject is tantamount to a quest for an unrestricted dislocation and the total disintegration of the social fabric. It also means that a democratic society which has become a viable social order will not be a totally free society, but one which has negotiated in a specific way the duality freedom/unfreedom.

2

Universalism, Particularism and the Question of Identity

There is today a lot of talk about social, ethnic, national and political identities. The 'death of the subject', which was proudly proclaimed *urbi et orbi* not so long ago, has been succeeded by a new and widespread interest in the multiple identities that are emerging and proliferating in our contemporary world. These two movements are not, however, in such a complete and dramatic contrast as we would be tempted to believe at first sight. Perhaps the death of *the* Subject (with a capital 'S') has been the main precondition of this renewed interest in the question of subjectivity. It is perhaps the very impossibility of any longer referring the concrete and finite expressions of a multifarious subjectivity to a transcendental centre that makes it possible to concentrate our attention on the multiplicity itself. The founding gestures of the 1960s are still with us, making possible the political and theoretical explorations in which we are today engaged.

If there was, however, this temporal gap between what had become theoretically thinkable and what was actually achieved, it is because a second and more subtle temptation haunted the intellectual imaginary of the Left for a while: that of replacing the transcendental subject with its symmetrical other, that of reinscribing the multifarious forms of undomesticated subjectivities in an objective totality. From this derived a concept which had a great deal of currency in our immediate prehistory: that of 'subject positions'. But this was not, of course, a real transcending of the problematic of transcendental subjectivity (something which haunts us as an absence is, indeed, very much present). 'History is a process without a subject'. Perhaps. But how do we know it? Is not the very possibility of such an assertion already requiring what one was trying to avoid? If history as a totality is a possible object of experience and discourse, who could be the subject of such an experience but the subject of an absolute knowledge? Now, if we try to avoid this pitfall, and negate the terrain that would make that assertion a meaningful one, what becomes problematic is the very notion of 'subject position'.

What could such a position be but a special location within a totality, and what could this totality be but the object of experience of an absolute subject? At the very moment in which the terrain of absolute subjectivity collapses, it also collapses *the very possibility* of an absolute object. There is no real alternative between Spinoza and Hegel. But this locates us in a very different terrain: one in which the very possibility of the subject/object distinction is the simple result of the impossibility of constituting either of its two terms. I am a subject precisely *because* I cannot be an absolute consciousness, because something constitutively alien confronts me; and there can be no pure object as a result of this opaqueness/alienation which shows the traces of the subject in the object. Thus, once objectivism disappeared as an 'epistemological obstacle', it became possible to develop the full implications of the 'death of the subject'. At that point, the latter showed the secret poison that inhabited it, the possibility of its second death: 'the death of the death of the subject'; the re-emergence of the subject as a result of its own death; the proliferation of concrete finitudes whose limitations are the source of their strength; the realization that there can be 'subjects' because the gap that 'the Subject' was supposed to bridge is actually unbridgeable.

This is not just abstract speculation; it is instead an intellectual way opened by the very terrain in which history has thrown us: the multiplication of new – and not so new – identities as a result of the collapse of the places from which the universal subjects spoke – the explosion of ethnic and national identities in Eastern Europe and in the territories of the former USSR, struggles of immigrant groups in Western Europe, new forms of multicultural protest and self-assertion in the USA, to which we have to add the gamut of forms of contestation associated with the new social movements. Now, the question arises: is this proliferation thinkable *just as* proliferation – that is, simply in terms of its multiplicity? To put the problem in its simplest terms: is particularism thinkable *just as* particularism, only out of the differential dimension that it asserts? Are the relations between universalism and particularism simple relations of mutual exclusion? Or, if we address the matter from the opposite angle: does the alternative between an essential objectivism and a transcendental subjectivism exhaust the range of language games that it is possible to play with the 'universal'?

These are the main questions that I am going to address. I will not pretend that the *place* of questioning does not affect the nature of the questions, and that the latter do not predetermine the kind of answer to be expected. Not all roads lead to Rome. But by confessing the tendentious nature of my intervention, I am giving the reader the only freedom that it is in my power to grant: that of stepping outside of my discourse and rejecting its validity in terms which are entirely incommensurable with it. So, in offering you some surfaces of inscription for the formulation of *questions* rather than answers, I am engaging in a power struggle for which there is a name: hegemony.

Let us start by considering the historical forms in which the relationship between universality and particularity has been thought. A first approach asserts: (a) that there is an uncontaminated dividing line between the universal and the particular; and (b) that the pole of the universal is entirely graspable by reason. In that case, there is no possible mediation between universality and particularity: the particular can only *corrupt* the universal. We are in the terrain of classical ancient philosophy. Either the particular realizes in itself the universal – that is it eliminates itself as particular and transforms itself in a transparent medium through which universality operates – or it negates the universal by asserting its particularism (but as the latter is purely irrational, it has no entity of its own and can only exist as corruption of being). The obvious question concerns the frontier dividing universality and particularity: is it universal or particular? If the latter, universality can only be a particularity which defines itself in terms of a limitless exclusion; if the former, the particular itself becomes part of the universal and the dividing line is again blurred. But the very possibility of formulating this last question would require that the *form* of universality as such is subjected to a clear differentiation from the actual *contents* to which it is associated. The thought of this difference, however, is not available to ancient philosophy.

The second possibility in thinking of the relation between

universality and particularity is related to Christianity. A point of view of the totality exists but it is God's, not ours, so that it is not accessible to human reason. *Credo quia absurdum*. Thus, the universal is mere event in an eschatological succession, only accessible to us through revelation. This involves an entirely different conception of the relationship between particularity and universality. The dividing line cannot be, as in ancient thought, that between rationality and irrationality, between a deep and a superficial layer *within the thing*, but that between two series of events: those of a finite and contingent succession on the one hand, and those of the eschatological series on the other. Because the designs of God are inscrutable, the deep layer cannot be a timeless world of rational forms, but a temporal succession of essential events which are opaque to human reason; and because each of these universal moments has to realize itself in a finite reality which has no common measure with them, the relation between the two orders also has to be an opaque and incomprehensible one. This type of relation was called incarnation, its distinctive feature being that between the universal and the body incarnating it there is no rational connection whatsoever. God is the only and absolute mediator. A subtle logic destined to have a profound influence on our intellectual tradition was started in this way: that of the *privileged agent of history*, the agent whose particular body was the expression of a universality transcending it. The modern idea of a 'universal class' and the various forms of Eurocentrism are nothing but the distant historical effects of the logic of incarnation.

Not entirely so, however, because modernity at its highest point was, to a large extent, the attempt to interrupt the logic of incarnation. God, as the absolute source of everything existing, was replaced in its function of universal guarantor by reason, but a *rational* ground and source has a logic of its own, which is very different from that of a divine intervention – the main difference being that the effects of a rational grounding have to be fully transparent to human reason. Now, this requirement is entirely incompatible with the logic of incarnation; if everything has to be transparent to reason, the connection between the universal and the body incarnating it also has to be so; in that case, the incommensurability between the universal to be incarnated and the incarnating body has to be eliminated. We have to postulate a body which is, in and of itself, the universal.

The full realization of these implications took several centuries. Descartes postulated a dualism in which the ideal of a full rationality still refused to become a principle of reorganization of the social and political world; but the main currents of the Enlightenment were going to establish a sharp frontier between the past, which was the realm of mistakes and follies of men, and a rational future, which had to be the result of an act of absolute institution. A last stage in the advance of this rationalistic hegemony took place when the gap between the rational and the irrational was closed through the representation of the act of its cancellation as a necessary moment in the self-development of reason: this was the task of Hegel and Marx, who asserted the total transparency, in absolute knowledge, of the real to reason. The body of the proletariat is no longer a particular body in which a universality external to it has to be incarnated: it is instead a body in which the distinction between particularity and universality is cancelled and, as a result, the need for any incarnation is definitely eradicated.

This was the point, however, at which social reality refused to abandon its resistance to universalistic rationalism. For an unsolved problem still remained. The universal had found its own body, but this was still the body of a certain particularity – European culture of the nineteenth century. So European culture was a particular one, and at the same time the expression – no longer the incarnation – of universal human essence (as the USSR was going to be considered later the 'motherland' of socialism). The crucial issue here is that there was no intellectual means of distinguishing between European particularism and the universal functions that it was supposed to incarnate, given that European universalism had constructed its identity precisely through the cancellation of the logic of incarnation and, as a result, through the universalization of its own particularism. So, European imperialist expansion had to be presented in terms of a universal civilizing function, modernization and so forth. The resistances of other cultures were, as a result, presented not as struggles between particular identities and cultures, but as part of an all-embracing and epochal struggle between universality and particularisms – the notion of peoples without history expressing precisely their incapacity to represent the universal.

This argument could be conceived in very explicit racist terms, as in the various forms of social Darwinism, but it could also be given some more 'progressive' versions – as in some sectors of the Second International – by asserting that the civilizing mission of Europe would finish with the establishment of a universally freed society of planetary dimensions. Thus, the logic of incarnation was reintroduced – Europe having to represent, for a certain period, universal human interests. In the case of Marxism, a similar reintroduction of the logic of incarnation takes place. Between the universal character of the tasks of the working class and the particularity of its concrete demands an increasing gap opened, which had to be filled by the Party as representative of the historical interests of the proletariat. The gap between class itself and class for itself opened the way to a succession of substitutions: the Party replaced the class, the autocrat the Party, and so on. Now, this well-known migration of the universal through the successive bodies incarnating it differed in one crucial point from Christian incarnation. In the latter a supernatural power was responsible both for the advent of the universal event and for the body which had to incarnate the latter. Human beings were on an equal footing *vis-à-vis* a power that transcended all of them. In the case of a secular eschatology, however, as the source of the universal is not external but internal to the world, the universal can only manifest itself through the establishment of an *essential* inequality between the objective positions of the social agents. Some of them are going to be privileged agents of historical change, not as a result of a contingent relation of forces but because they are incarnations of the universal. The same type of logic operating in Eurocentrism will establish the ontological privilege of the proletariat.

As this ontological privilege is the result of a process which was conceived as entirely rational, it was doubled into an epistemological privilege: the point of view of the proletariat supersedes the opposition subject/object. In a classless society, social relations will finally be fully transparent. It is true that if the increasing simplification of the social structure under capitalism had taken place in the way predicted by Marx, the consequences of this approach would not necessarily have been authoritarian, because the position of the proletariat as bearer of the viewpoint of social totality and the position of the vast majority of the population would have overlapped. But if the process moved – as it did – in the opposite direction, the successive bodies incarnating the viewpoint of the universal class had to have an increasingly restricted social base. The vanguard party, as concrete particularity, had to claim to have knowledge of the 'objective meaning' of any event, and the viewpoint of the other particular social forces had to be dismissed as false consciousness. From this point on, the authoritarian turn was unavoidable.

This whole story is apparently leading to an inevitable conclusion: the chasm between the universal and the particular is unbridgeable – which is the same as saying that the universal is no more than a particular that at some moment has become dominant, that there is no way of reaching a reconciled society. And, in actual fact, the spectacle of the social and political struggles of the 1990s seems to confront us, as we said before, with a proliferation of particularisms, while the point of view of universality is increasingly put aside as an old-fashioned totalitarian dream. However, I will argue that an appeal to pure particularism is no solution to the problems that we are facing in contemporary societies. In the first place, the assertion of pure particularism, independently of any content and of the appeal to a universality transcending it, is a self-defeating enterprise. For if it is the only accepted normative principle, it confronts us with an unsolvable paradox. I can defend the right of sexual, racial and national minorities in the name of particularism; but if particularism is the only valid principle, I have to also accept the rights to self-determination of all kinds of reactionary groups involved in antisocial practices. Even more: as the demands of various groups will necessarily clash with each other, we have to appeal – short of postulating some kind of pre-established harmony – to some more general principles in order to regulate such clashes. In actual fact, there is no particularism which does not make appeal to such principles in the construction of its own identity. These principles can be progressive in our appreciation, such as the right of peoples to self-determination – or reactionary, such as social Darwinism or the right to *Lebensraum* – but they are always there, and for essential reasons.

There is a second and perhaps more important reason why pure particularism is self-defeating. Let us accept, for the sake of the argument, that the above-mentioned pre-established harmony is possible. In that case, the various particularisms

26

would not be in antagonistic relation with each other, but would coexist one with the other in a coherent whole. This hypothesis shows clearly why the argument for pure particularism is ultimately inconsistent. For if each identity is in a differential, non-antagonistic relation to all other identities, then the identity in question is purely differential and relational; so it presupposes not only the presence of all the other identities but also the total ground which constitutes the differences as differences. Even worse: we know very well that the relations between groups are constituted as relations of power – that is, that each group is not only different from the others but constitutes in many cases such difference on the basis of the exclusion and subordination of other groups. Now, if the particularity asserts itself as mere particularity, in a purely differential relation with other partic-ularities, it is sanctioning the *status quo* in the relation of power between the groups. This is exactly the notion of 'separate developments' as formulated in apartheid: only the differential aspect is stressed, while the relations of power on which the latter is based are systematically ignored.

This last example is important because, coming from a discursive universe – South African apartheid – which is quite opposite to that of the new particularisms that we are discussing, and revealing, however, the same ambiguities in the construction of any difference, it opens the way to an understanding of a dimension of the relationship particularism/universalism which has generally been disregarded. The basic point is this: I cannot assert a differential identity without distinguishing it from a context, and, in the process of making the distinction, I am asserting the context at the same time. And the opposite is also true: I cannot destroy a context without destroying at the same time the identity of the particular subject who carries out the destruction. It is a very well known historical fact that an oppositionist force whose identity is constructed within a certain system of power is ambiguous *vis-à-vis* that system, because the latter is what prevents the constitution of the identity and it is, at the same time, its condition of existence. And any victory against the system also destabilizes the identity of the victorious force.

Now, an important corollary of this argument is that if a fully achieved difference eliminates the antagonistic dimension as constitutive of any identity, the possibility of maintaining this dimension depends on the very failure in the full constitution of a differential identity. It is here that the 'universal' enters into the scene. Let us suppose that we are dealing with the constitution of the identity of an ethnic minority for instance. As we said earlier, if this differential identity is fully achieved, it can only be so within a context – for instance, a nation-state – and the price to be paid for total victory *within the context* is total integration with it. If, on the contrary, total integration *does not* take place, it is because that identity is not fully achieved – there are, for instance, unsatisfied demands concerning access to education, to employment, to consumer goods and so on. These demands cannot be made in terms of difference, but of some universal principles that the ethnic minority shares with the rest of the community: the right of everybody to have access to good schools, or live a decent life, or participate in the public space of citizenship, and so on.

This means that the universal is part of my identity as far as I am penetrated by a constitutive lack, that is as far as my differential identity has failed in its process of constitution. The universal emerges out of the particular not as some principle underlying and explaining the particular, but as an incomplete horizon suturing a dislocated particular identity. This points to a way of conceiving the relations between the universal and the particular which is different from those that we have explored earlier. In the case of the logic of incarnation, the universal and the particular were fully constituted but totally separated identities, whose connection was the result of a divine intervention, impenetrable to human reason. In the case of secularized eschatologies, the particular had to be eliminated entirely: the universal class was conceived as the cancellation of all differences. In the case of extreme particularism there is no universal body – but, as the ensemble of non-antagonistic particularities purely and simply reconstructs the notion of social totality, the classical notion of the universal is not put into question in the least. (A universal conceived as a homogeneous space differentiated by its internal articulations and a *system* of differences constituting a unified ensemble are exactly the same.) Now we are pointing to a fourth alternative: the universal is the symbol of a missing fullness and the particular exists only in the contradictory movement of asserting at the same time a differential identity and cancelling it through its subsumption in the non-differential medium.

I will devote the rest of this paper to discussing three important political conclusions that one can derive from this fourth alternative. The first is that the construction of differential identities on the basis of total closure to what is outside them is not a viable or progressive political alternative. It would be a reactionary policy in Western Europe today, for instance, for immigrants from Northern Africa or Jamaica to abstain from all participation in Western European institutions, with the justification that theirs is a different cultural identity and that European institutions are not their concern. In this way, all forms of subordination and exclusion would be consolidated with the excuse of maintaining pure identities. The logic of apartheid is not only a discourse of the dominant groups; as we said before, it can also permeate the identities of the oppressed. At its very limit, understood as *mere* difference, the discourse of the oppressor and the discourse of the oppressed cannot be distinguished. The reason for this we have given earlier: if the oppressed is defined by its difference from the oppressor, such a difference is an essential component of the identity of the oppressed. But in that case, the latter cannot assert its identity without asserting that of the oppressor as well:

> Il y a bien des dangers à invoquer des différences pures, libérées de l'identique, devenues independantes du négatif. Le plus grand danger est de tomber dans les représentations de la belle-âme: rien que des différences, conciliables et fédérables, loin des luttes sanglantes. La belle-âme dit: nous sommes différentes, main non pas opposés.[1]

The idea of 'negative' implicit in the dialectical notion of contradiction is unable to take us beyond this conservative logic of pure difference. A negative which is part of the determination of a positive content is an integral part of the latter. This is what shows the two faces of Hegel's *Logic*: if, on the one hand, the inversion defining the speculative proposition means that the predicate becomes subject, and that a universality transcending all particular determinations 'circulates' through the latter, on the other hand, that circulation has a direction dictated by the movement of the particular determinations themselves, and is strictly reduced to it. Dialectical negativity does not question in the least the logic of identity (= the logic of pure difference).

This shows the ambiguity which is inherent in all forms of radical opposition: the opposition, in order to be radical, has to

29

put in a common ground both what it asserts and what it excludes, so that the exclusion becomes a particular form of assertion. But this means that a particularism really committed to change can only do so by rejecting both what denies its own identity and that identity itself. There is no clear-cut solution to the paradox of radically negating a system of power while remaining in secret dependency on it. It is well known how opposition to certain forms of power requires identification with the very places from which the opposition takes place; as the latter are, however, internal to the opposed system, there is a certain conservatism inherent in *all* opposition. The reason why this is unavoidable is that the ambiguity inherent in *all* antagonistic relation is something we can negotiate with but not actually supersede – we can play with both sides of the ambiguity and produce results by preventing any of them prevailing in an exclusive way, but the ambiguity as such cannot be properly *resolved*. To surpass an ambiguity involves going beyond both its poles, but this means that there can be no simple politics of preservation of an identity. If the racial or cultural minority, for instance, has to assert its identity in new social surroundings, it will have to take into account new situations which will inevitably transform that identity. This means, of course, moving away from the idea of negation as radical reversal.[2] The main consequence that follows is that, if the politics of difference means continuity of difference by being always an *other*, the rejection of the other cannot be radical elimination either, but constant renegotiation of the forms of his presence. Aletta J. Norval asked herself recently about identities in a post-apartheid society:

> The question looming on the horizon is this: what are the implications of recognizing that the identity of the other is constitutive of the self, in a situation where apartheid itself will have become something of the past? That is, how do we think of social and political identities as post-apartheid?

And after asserting that:

> [I]f the other is merely rejected, externalized *in toto* in the movement in which apartheid receives its signified, we would have effected a reversal of the order, remaining in effect in the terrain in which apartheid has organized and ruled . . .

30

she points to a different possibility:

> Through a remembrance of apartheid as other, post-apartheid could become the site from which the final closure and suturing of identities is to be prevented. Paradoxically, a post-apartheid society will then only be radically beyond apartheid in so far as apartheid itself is present in it as its other. Instead of being effaced once and for all, 'apartheid' itself would have to play the role of the element keeping open the relation to the other, of serving as watchword against any discourse claiming to be able to create a final unity.[3]

This argument can be generalized. Everything hinges on which of the two equally possible movements leading to the suppression of oppression is initiated. None can avoid maintaining the reference to the 'other', but they do so in two completely different ways. If we simply *invert* the relation of oppression, the other (the former oppressor) is maintained as what is now oppressed and repressed, but this inversion of the *contents* leaves the form of oppression unchanged. And as the identity of the newly emancipated groups has been constituted through the rejection of the old dominant ones, the latter continue shaping the identity of the former. The operation of inversion takes place entirely within the old *formal* system of power. But as we have seen, all political identity is internally split, because no particularity can be constituted except by maintaining an internal reference to universality as that which is missing. But in that case, the identity of the oppressor will equally be split: on the one hand, he will represent a particular system of oppression; on the other, he will symbolize the *form* of oppression as such. This is what makes the second move suggested in Norval's text possible: instead of inverting a particular relation of oppression/closure in what it has of concrete particularity, inverting it in what it has of universality: the *form* of oppression and closure as such. The reference to the other is also maintained here but, as the inversion takes place at the level of the universal reference and not of the concrete contents of an oppressive system, the identities of *both* oppressors and oppressed are radically changed. A similar argument was made by Walter Benjamin with reference to Sorel's distinction between political strike and proletarian strike: while the political strike aims at obtaining concrete reforms that change a system of power and thereby constitute a new power, the proletarian strike aims at the destruction of power as such, of the very form of power, and in this sense it does not have any particular objective.[4]

These remarks allow us to throw some light on the divergent courses of action that current struggles in defence of multi-culturalism can follow. One possible way is to affirm, purely and simply, the right of the various cultural and ethnic groups to assert their differences and their separate development. This is the route to self-apartheid, and it is sometimes accompanied by the claim that Western cultural values and institutions are the preserve of white, male Europeans or Anglo-Americans and have nothing to do with the identity of other groups living in the same territory. What is advocated in this way is total segregation-ism, the mere opposition of one particularism to another. Now, it is true that the assertion of any particular identity involves, as one of its dimensions, the affirmation of the right to a separate existence. But it is here that the difficult questions start, because the separation – or better, the right to difference – has to be asserted within the global community – that is within a space in which that particular group has to coexist with other groups. Now, how could that coexistence be possible without some shared universal values, without a sense of belonging to a community larger than each of the particular groups in question? Here people sometimes say that any agreement should be reached through *negotiation*. Negotiation, however, is an ambiguous term that can mean very different things. One of these is a process of mutual pressures and concessions whose outcome depends only on the balance of power between antagonistic groups. It is obvious that no sense of community can be constructed through that type of negotiation. The relation between groups can only be one of potential war. *Vis pacis para bellum*. This is not far away from the conception of the nature of the agreement between groups implicit in the Leninist conception of class alliances: the agreement concerns only circumstantial matters, but the identity of the forces entering it remains uncontaminated by the process of negotiation. Translated into the cultural field, this affirmation of an extreme separatism led to the sharp distinction between bourgeois science and proletarian science. Gramsci was well aware that, in spite of the extreme diversity of the social forces that had to enter into the construction of a hegemonic identity, no collective will and no sense of community could result from such a conception of negotiation and alliances.

The dilemma of the defenders of extreme particularism is that their political action is anchored in a perpetual incoherence. On the one hand, they defend the right to difference as a universal right, and this defence involves their engagement in struggles for changes in legislation, for the protection of minorities in courts, against the violation of civil rights, and so forth. That is they are engaged in a struggle for the internal reform of the present institutional setting. But on the other hand, as they simultaneously assert both that this setting is necessarily rooted in the cultural and political values of the traditional dominant sectors of the West *and that they have nothing to do with that tradition*, their demands cannot be articulated into any wider hegemonic operation to reform the system. This condemns them to an ambiguous peripheral relation with the existing institutions, which can have only paralyzing political effects.

This is not, however, the only possible course of action for those engaged in particularistic struggles – and this is our second conclusion. As we have seen before, a system of oppression (that is of closure) can be combated in two different ways – either by an operation of inversion which performs a new closure, or by negating in that system its universal dimension: the principle of closure as such. It is one thing to say that the universalistic values of the West are the preserve of its traditional dominant groups; it is very different to assert that the historical link between the two is a contingent and unacceptable fact which can be modified through political and social struggles. When Mary Wollstonecraft, in the wake of the French Revolution, defended the rights of women, she did not present the exclusion of women from the declaration of the rights of man and citizen as a proof that the latter are intrinsically male rights, but tried, on the contrary, to deepen the democratic revolution by showing the incoherence of establishing universal rights which were restricted to particular sectors of the population. The democratic process in present-day societies can be considerably deepened and expanded if it is made accountable to the demands of large sections of the population – minorities, ethnic groups and so on – who traditionally have been excluded from it. Liberal democratic theory and institutions have in this sense, to be deconstructed. As they were originally thought for societies which were far more homogeneous than the present ones, they were based on all kinds of unexpressed assumptions which no longer obtain in the present situation. Present-day social and political struggles can bring to the fore this game of decisions taken in an undecidable terrain, and help us to move in the direction of new democratic practices and a new democratic theory which is fully adapted to the present circumstances. That political participation can lead to political and social integration is certainly true, but for the reasons we gave before, political and cultural segregation can lead to exactly the same result. Anyway, the decline of the integrationist abilities of the Western states make political conformism a rather unlikely outcome. I would argue that the unresolved tension between universalism and particularism opens the way to a movement away from Western Eurocentrism, through the operation that we could call a systematic decentring of the West. As we have seen, Eurocentrism was the result of a discourse which did not differentiate between the universal values that the West was advocating and the concrete social agents that were incarnating them. Now, however, we can proceed to a separation of these two aspects. If social struggles of new social actors show that the concrete practices of our society restrict the universalism of our political ideals to limited sectors of the population, it becomes possible to retain the universal dimension while widening the spheres of its application – which, in turn, will define the concrete contents of such universality. Through this process, universalism as a horizon is expanded at the same time as its necessary attachment to any particular content is broken. The opposite policy – that of rejecting universalism *in toto* as the particular content of the ethnia of the West – can only lead to a political blind alley.

This leaves us, however, with an apparent paradox – and its analysis will be my last conclusion. The universal, as we have seen, does not have a concrete content of its own (which would close it on itself), but is an always receding horizon resulting from the expansion of an indefinite chain of equivalent demands. The conclusion seems to be that universality is incommensurable with any particularity but cannot, however, exist apart from the particular. In terms of our previous analysis: if only particular actors, or constellations of particular actors can actualize the universal at any moment, in that case, the possibility of making visible the nonclosure inherent to a post-dominated society – that is a society that attempts to transcend the very form of domination – depends on making the asymmetry between the universal and the particular permanent. The universal is incommensurable with the particular, but cannot, however, exist without the latter. How is this relation possible? My answer is that this paradox cannot be solved, but that its non-solution is the very precondition of democracy. The solution of the paradox would imply that a particular body had been found, which would be the *true* body of the universal. But in that case, the universal would have found its necessary location, and democracy would be impossible. If democracy is possible, it is because the universal has no necessary body and no necessary content; different groups, instead, compete between themselves to temporarily give to their particularisms a function of universal representation. Society generates a whole vocabulary of empty signifiers whose temporary signifieds are the result of a political competition. It is this final failure of society to constitute itself as society – which is the same thing as the failure of constituting difference as difference – which makes the distance between the universal and the particular unbridgeable and, as a result, burdens concrete social agents with the impossible task of making democratic interaction achievable.

Notes

1. Gilles Deleuze, *Différence et Répétition*, Paris, Presses Universitaires de France 1989, p. 2.

2. It is at this point that, in my recent work, I have tried to complement the idea of radical antagonism – which still involves the possibility of a radical representability – with the notion of dislocation which is previous to any kind of antagonistic representation. Some of the dimensions of this duality have been explored by Bobby Sayyid and Lilian Zac in a short, written presentation to a Ph.D. seminar on Ideology and Discourse Analysis, University of Essex, December 1990.

3. Aletta J. Norval, 'Letter to Ernesto', in Ernesto Laclau, *New Reflections on the Revolution of our Time*, London, Verso 1990, p. 157.

4. Cf. Walter Benjamin, 'Zur Kritik der Gewalt', in R. Tiedemann and H. Schweppenhauser (eds.), *Gesemmelte Schriften*, 179, 1977. See a commentary on Benjamin's text in Werner Hamacher, 'Afformative, Strike', *Cardozo Law Review*, vol. 13, no. 4, December 1991.

3

Why do Empty Signifiers Matter to Politics?

The Social Production of 'Empty Signifiers'

An empty signifier is, strictly speaking, a signifier without a signified. This definition is also, however, the enunciation of a problem. For how would it be possible that a signifier is not attached to any signified and remains, nevertheless, an integral part of a system of signification? An empty signifier would be a sequence of sounds, and if the latter are deprived of any signifying function the term 'signifier' itself would become excessive. The only possibility for a stream of sounds being detached from any particular signified while still remaining a signifier is if, through the subversion of the sign which the possibility of an empty signifier involves, something is achieved which is internal to significations as such. What is this possibility?

Some pseudo answers can be discarded quite quickly. One would be to argue that the same signifier can be attached to different signifieds in different contexts (as a result of the arbitrariness of the sign). But it is clear that, in that case, the signifier would not be *empty* but *equivocal*: the function of signification in each context would be fully realised. A second possibility is that the signifier is not *equivocal* but *ambiguous*: that either an overdetermination or an underdetermination of signifieds prevents it from being fully fixed. Yet this floating of the signifier still does not make it an empty one. Although the floating takes us one step towards the proper answer to our problem, the terms of the latter are still avoided. We do not have to deal with an excess or deficiency of signification, but with the precise theoretical possibility of something which points, from within the process of signification, to the discursive presence of its own limits.

An empty signifier can, consequently, only emerge if there is a structural impossibility in signification as such, and only if this impossibility can signify itself as an interruption (subversion, distortion, etcetera) of the structure of the sign. That is, the limits of signification can only announce themselves as the impossibility of realizing what is within those limits – if the limits could be signified in a direct way, they would be internal to signification and, *ergo*, would not be limits at all.

An initial and purely formal consideration can help to clarify the point. We know, from Saussure, that language (and by extension, all signifying systems) is a system of differences, that linguistic identities – values – are purely relational and that, as a result, the totality of language is involved in each single act of signification. Now, in that case, it is clear that the totality is essentially required – if the differences did not constitute a system, no signification at all would be possible. The problem, however, is that the very possibility of signification is the system, and the very possibility of the system is the possibility of its limits. We can say, with Hegel, that to think of the limits of something is the same as thinking of what is beyond those limits. But if what we are talking about are the limits of a *signifying system*, it is clear that those limits cannot be themselves signified, but have to *show* themselves as the *interruption* or *breakdown* of the process of signification. Thus, we are left with the paradoxical situation that what constitutes the condition of possibility of a signifying system – its limits – is also what constitutes its condition of impossibility – a blockage of the continuous expansion of the process of signification.

A first and capital consequence of this is that true limits can never be neutral limits but presuppose an exclusion. A neutral limit would be one which is essentially continuous with what is at its two sides, and the two sides are simply different from each other. As a signifying totality is, however, precisely a system of differences, this means that both are part of the same system and that the limits between the two cannot be the limits of the system. In the case of an exclusion we have, instead, authentic limits because the actualization of what is beyond the limit of exclusion would involve the impossibility of what is this side of the limit. True limits are always antagonistic. But the operation of the logic of exclusionary limits has a series of necessary effects which spread to both sides of the limits and which will lead us straight into the emergence of empty signifiers:

1. A first effect of the exclusionary limit is that it introduces an essential ambivalence within the system of differences constituted by those limits. On the one hand, each element of the system has an identity only so far as it is different from the others: difference = identity. On the other hand, however, all these differences are equivalent to each other inasmuch as all of them belong to this side of the frontier of exclusion. But, in that case, the identity of each element is constitutively split: on the one hand, each difference expresses itself *as* difference; on the other hand, each of them *cancels* itself as such by entering into a relation of equivalence with all the other differences of the system. And, given that there is only system as long as there is radical exclusion, this split or ambivalence is constitutive of all systemic identity. It is only in so far as there is a radical impossibility of a system as pure presence, beyond all exclusions, that actual *systems* (in the plural) can exist. Now, if the systematicity of the system is a direct result of the exclusionary limit, it is only that exclusion that grounds the system as such. This point is essential because it results from it that the system cannot have a positive ground and that, as a result, it cannot signify itself in terms of any positive signified. Let us suppose for a moment that the systematic ensemble was the result of all its elements sharing a positive feature (for example that they all belonged to a regional category). In that case, that positive feature would be different from other differential positive features, and they would all appeal to a deeper systematic ensemble within which their differences would be thought of as differences. But a system constituted through radical exclusion interrupts this play of the differential logic: what is excluded from the system, far from being something positive, is the simple principle of positivity – pure being. This already announces the possibility of an empty signifier – that is a signifier of the pure cancellation of all difference.

2. The condition, of course, for this operation to be possible is that what is beyond the frontier of exclusion is reduced to pure negativity – that is to the pure threat that what is beyond poses to the system (constituting it that way). If the exclusionary dimension was eliminated, or even weakened, what would happen is that the differential character of the 'beyond' would impose itself and, as a result, the limits of the system would be blurred. Only if the beyond becomes the signifier of pure threat, of pure negativity, of the simply excluded, can there be limits and system (that is an objective order). But in order to be the signifiers of the excluded (or, simply of

exclusion), the various excluded categories have to cancel their differences through the formation of a chain of equivalences to that which the system demonizes in order to signify itself. Again, we see here the possibility of an empty signifier announcing itself through this logic in which differences collapse into equivalential chains.

3. But, we could ask ourselves, why does this pure being or systematicity of the system, or – its reverse – the pure negativity of the excluded, require the production of empty signifiers in order to signify itself? The answer is that we are trying to signify the limits of signification – the real, if you want, in the Lacanian sense – and there is no direct way of doing so except through the subversion of the process of signification itself. We know, through psychoanalysis, how what is not directly representable – the unconscious – can only find as a means of representation the subversion of the signifying process. Each signifier constitutes a sign by attaching itself to a particular signified, inscribing itself as a difference within the signifying process. But if what we are trying to signify is not a difference but, on the contrary, a radical exclusion which is the ground and condition of all differences, in that case, no production of *one more* difference can do the trick. As, however, all the means of representation are differential in nature, it is only if the differential nature of the signifying units is subverted, only if the signifiers empty themselves of their attachment to particular signifieds and assume the role of representing the pure being of the system – or, rather, the system as pure Being – that such a signification is possible. What is the ontological ground of such subversion, what makes it possible? The answer is: the split of each unit of signification that the system has to construct as the undecidable locus in which both the logic of difference and the logic of equivalence operate. It is only by privileging the dimension of equivalence to the point that its differential nature is almost entirely obliterated – that is emptying it of its differential nature – that the system can signify itself as a totality.

Two points have to be stressed here. The first is that the being or systematicity of the system which is represented through the empty signifiers is not a being which has not been *actually* realized, but one which is constitutively unreachable, for whatever systematic effects that would exist will be the result, as we have seen, of the unstable compromise between equivalence and difference. That is, we are faced with a constitutive lack, with an impossible object which, as in Kant, shows itself through the impossibility of its adequate representation. Here, we can give a full answer to our initial question: there can be empty signifiers within the field of signification because any system of signification is structured around an empty place resulting from the impossibility of producing an object which, none the less, is required by the systematicity of the system. So, we are not dealing with an impossibility without location, as in the case of a logical contradiction, but with a *positive* impossibility, with a *real* one to which the *x* of the empty signifier points.

However, if this impossible object lacks the means of its adequate or direct representation, this can only mean that the signifier which is emptied in order to assume the representing function will always be constitutively inadequate. What, in that case, does determine that one signifier rather than another assumes in different circumstances that signifying function? Here, we have to move to the main theme of this essay: the relation between empty signifiers and politics.

Hegemony

Let me go back to an example that we discussed in detail in *Hegemony and Socialist Strategy*:[1] the constitution, according to Rosa Luxemburg, of the unity of the working class through an overdetermination of partial struggles over a long period of time. Her basic argument is that the unity of the class is not determined by an a priori consideration about the priority of either the political struggle or the economic struggle, but by the accumulated effects of the internal split of all partial mobilizations. In relation to our subject, her argument amounts to approximately the following: in a climate of extreme repression any mobilization for a partial objective will be perceived not only as related to the concrete demand or objectives of that struggle, but also as an act of opposition against the system. This last fact is what establishes the link between a variety of concrete or partial struggles and mobilizations – all of them are seen as related to each other, not because their concrete objectives are intrinsically related but because they are all seen as equivalent in confrontation with the repressive regime. It is not, consequently, something positive that all of them share which establishes their unity, but something negative: their opposition to a common enemy. Luxemburg's argument is that a revolutionary mass identity is established through the overdetermination, over a whole historical period, of a plurality of separate struggles. These traditions fused, at the revolutionary moment, in a ruptural point.

Let us try to apply our previous categories to this sequence. The meaning (the signified) of all concrete struggles appears, right from the beginning, internally divided. The concrete aim of the struggle is not only that aim in its concreteness; it also signifies opposition to the system. The first signified establishes the differential character of that demand or mobilization *vis-à-vis* all other demands or mobilizations. The second signified establishes the equivalence of all these demands in their common opposition to the system. As we can see, any concrete struggle is dominated by this contradictory movement that simultaneously asserts and abolishes its own singularity. The function of representing the system as a totality depends, consequently, on the possibility of the equivalential function neatly prevailing over the differential one; but this possibility is simply the result of every single struggle always being already, originally, penetrated by this constitutive ambiguity.

It is important to observe that, as we have already established, if the function of the differential signifiers is to renounce their differential identity in order to represent the purely equivalential identity of a communitarian space as such, they cannot construct this equivalential identity as something belonging to a differential order. For instance: we can represent the Tzarist regime as a repressive order by enumerating the differential kinds of oppression that it imposed on various sections of the population as much as we want; but such enumeration will not give us the specificity of the repressive moment, that which constitutes – in its negation – what is peculiar to a repressive relation between entities. Because in such a relation each instance of the repressive power counts as pure bearer of the negation of the identity of the repressed sector. Now, if the differential identity of the repressive action is in that way 'distanced' from itself by having itself transformed into the mere incarnating body of the negation of the being of another entity, it is clear that between this negation and the body through which it expresses itself there is no necessary relation – nothing predetermines that one particular body should be the one predestined to incarnate negation as such.

It is precisely this which makes the relation of equivalence possible: different particular struggles are so many bodies which can indifferently incarnate the opposition of all of them to the repressive power. This involves a double movement. On the one hand, the more the chain of equivalences is extended, the less each concrete struggle will be able to remain closed in a differential self – in something which separates it from all other differential identities through a difference which is exclusively its own. On the contrary, as the equivalent relation shows that these differential identities are simply indifferent bodies incarnating something equally present in all of them, the longer the chain of equivalences is, the less concrete this 'something equally present' will be. At the limit it will be pure communitarian being independent of all concrete manifestation. And, on the other hand, that which is beyond the exclusion delimiting the communitarian space – the repressive power – will count less as the instrument of particular differential repressions and will express pure anti-community, pure evil and negation. The community created by this equivalential expansion will be, thus, the pure idea of a communitarian fullness which is absent – as a result of the presence of the repressive power.

But, at this point, the second movement starts. This pure equivalential function representing an absent fullness which shows itself through the collapse of all differential identities is something which cannot have a signifier of its own – for in that case, the 'beyond all differences' would be one more difference and not the result of the equivalential collapse of all differential identities. Precisely because the community as such is not a purely differential space of an objective identity but an absent fullness, it cannot have any form of representation of its own, and has to borrow the latter from some entity constituted within the equivalential space – in the same way as gold is a particular use value which assumes, as well, the function of representing value in general. This emptying of a particular signifier of its particular, differential signified is, as we saw, what makes possible the emergence of 'empty' signifiers as the signifiers of a lack, of an absent totality. But this leads us straight into the question with which we closed the previous section: if all differential struggles – in our example – are equally capable of expressing, beyond their differential identity, the absent fullness of the community; if the equivalential function makes all differential positions similarly indifferent to this equivalential representation; if none is predetermined *per se* to fulfil this role; what does determine that one of them rather than another incarnates, at particular periods of time, this universal function?

The answer is: the unevenness of the social. For if the equivalential logic tends to do away with the relevance of all differential location, this is only a tendential movement that is always resisted by the logic of difference which is essentially non-equalitarian. (It comes as no surprise that Hobbes's model of a state of nature, which tries to depict a realm in which the full operation of the logic of equivalence makes the community impossible, has to presuppose an original and essential equality between men.) Not any position in society, not any struggle is equally capable of transforming its own contents in a nodal point that becomes an empty signifier. Now, is this not to return to a rather traditional conception of the historical effectivity of social forces, one which asserts that the unevenness of structural locations determines which one of them is going to be the source of totalizing effects? No, it is not, because these uneven structural locations, some of which represent points of high concentration of power, are themselves the result of processes in which logics of difference and logics of equivalence overdetermine each other. It is not a question of denying the historical effectivity of the logic of differential structural locations but, rather, of denying to them, as a whole, the character of an infrastructure which would determine, out of itself, the laws of movement of society.

If this is correct, it is impossible to determine at the level of the mere analysis of the *form* difference/equivalence which particular difference is going to become the locus of equivalential effects – this requires the study of a particular conjuncture, precisely because the presence of equivalential effects is always necessary, but the relation equivalence/difference is not intrinsically linked to any particular differential content. This relation by which a particular content becomes the signifier of the absent communitarian fullness is exactly what we call a *hegemonic relationship*. The presence of empty signifiers – in the sense that we have defined them – is the very condition of hegemony. This can be easily seen if we address a very well known difficulty which forms a recurring stumbling block in most theorizations of hegemony – Gramsci's included. A class or group is considered to be hegemonic when it is not closed in a narrow corporatist perspective, but presents itself as realizing the broader aims either of emancipating or ensuring order for wider masses of the population. But this faces us with a difficulty if we do not determine precisely what these terms '*broader* aims', '*wider* masses' refer to. There are two possibilities: first, that society is an addition of discrete groups, each tending to their particular aims and in constant collision with each other. In that case, 'broader' and 'wider' could only mean the precarious equilibrium of a negotiated agreement between groups, all of which would retain their conflicting aims and identity. But 'hegemony' clearly refers to a stronger type of communitarian unity than such an agreement evokes. Second, that society has some kind of pre-established essence, so that the 'broader' and 'wider' has a content of its own, independent of the will of the particular groups, and that 'hegemony' would mean the realization of such an essence. But this would not only do away with the dimension of contingency which has always been associated with the hegemonic operation, but would also be incompatible with the consensual character of 'hegemony': the hegemonic order would be the *imposition* of a pre-given organizational principle and not something emerging from the political interaction between groups. Now, if we consider the matter from the point of view of the social production of empty signifiers, this problem vanishes. For in that case, the hegemonic operations would be the presentation of the particularity of a group as the incarnation of that empty signifier which refers to the communitarian order as an absence, an unfulfilled reality.

How does this mechanism operate? Let us consider the extreme situation of a radical disorganization of the social fabric. In such conditions – which are not far away from Hobbes's state of nature – people need *an* order, and the actual content of it becomes a secondary consideration. 'Order' as such has no content, because it only exists in the various forms in which it is actually realized, but in a situation of radical disorder 'order' is present as that which is absent; it becomes an empty signifier, as the signifier of that absence. In this sense, various political forces can compete in their efforts to present their particular objectives as those which carry out the filling of that lack. To hegemonize something is exactly to carry out this filling function. (We have spoken about 'order', but obviously 'unity', 'liberation', 'revolution', etcetera belong to the same order of things. Any term which, in a certain political context becomes the signifier of the lack, plays the same role. Politics is possible because the constitutive impossibility of society can only represent itself through the production of empty signifiers.)

This explains also why any hegemony is always unstable and penetrated by a constitutive ambiguity. Let us suppose that a workers' mobilization succeeds in presenting its own objectives as a signifier of 'liberation' in general. (This, as we have seen, is possible because the workers' mobilization, taking place under a repressive regime, is also seen as an anti-system struggle.) In one sense this is a hegemonic victory, because the objectives of a particular group are identified with society at large. But, in another sense, this is a dangerous victory. If 'workers' struggle' becomes the signifier of liberation as such, it also becomes the surface of inscription through which *all* liberating struggles will be expressed, so that the chain of equivalences which are unified around this signifier tend to empty it, and to blur its connection with the actual content with which it was originally associated. Thus, as a result of its very success, the hegemonic operation tends to break its links with the force which was its original promoter and beneficiary.

Hegemony and Democracy

Let us conclude with some reflections on the relation between empty signifiers, hegemony and democracy.

Consider for a moment the role of social signifiers in the emergence of modern political thought – I am essentially thinking of the work of Hobbes. Hobbes, as we have seen, presented the state of nature as the radically opposite of an ordered society, as a situation only defined in negative terms. But, as a result of that description, the order of the ruler has to be accepted not because of any intrinsic virtue that it can have, but just because it is *an* order, and the only alternative is radical disorder. The condition, however, of the coherence of this scheme is the postulate of the equality of the power of individuals in the state of nature – if the individuals were uneven in terms of power, order could be guaranteed through sheer domination. So, power is eliminated twice: in the state of nature, as all individuals equally share in it, and in the commonwealth, as it is entirely concentrated in the hands of the ruler. (A power which is total or a power which is equally distributed among all members of the community is no power at all.) So, while Hobbes implicitly perceives the split between the empty signifier 'order as such' and the actual order imposed by the ruler, as he reduces – through the covenant – the first to the second, he cannot think of any kind of dialectical or hegemonic game between the two.

What happens if, on the contrary, we reintroduce power within the picture – that is if we accept the unevenness of power in social relations? In that case, civil society will be partially structured and partially unstructured and, as a result, the total concentration of power in the hands of the ruler ceases to be a logical requirement. But in that case, the credentials of the ruler to claim total power are much less obvious. If partial order exists in society, the legitimacy of the identification of the empty signifier of order with the will of the ruler will have the further requirement that the content of this will does not clash with something the society *already* is. As society changes over time this process of identification will be always precarious and reversible and, as the identification is no longer automatic, different projects or wills will try to hegemonize the empty signifiers of the absent community. The recognition of the constitutive nature of this gap and its political institutionalization is the starting point of modern democracy.

Note

1. Ernesto Laclau and Chantal Mouffe, *Hegemony and Socialist Strategy*, London, Verso 1985.

4

Subject of Politics, Politics of the Subject

The question of the relationship (complementarity? tension? mutual exclusion?) between universalism and particularism occupies a central place on the current political and theoretical agenda. Universal values are seen either as dead or – at the very least – as threatened. What is more important, the positive character of those values is no longer taken for granted. On the one hand, under the banner of multiculturalism, the classical values of the Enlightenment are under fire, and considered as little more than the cultural preserve of Western imperialism. On the other hand, the whole debate concerning the end of modernity, the assault on foundationalism in its various expressions, has tended to establish an essential link between the obsolete notion of a ground of history and society, and the *actual contents* which, from the Enlightenment onwards, have played that role of ground. It is important, however, to realize that these two debates have not advanced along symmetrical lines, that argumentative strategies have tended to move from one to the other in unexpected ways, and that many apparently paradoxical combinations have been shown to be possible. Thus, the so-called postmodern approaches can be seen as weakening the imperialist foundationalism of Western Enlightenment and opening the way to a more democratic cultural pluralism; but they can also be perceived as underpinning a notion of 'weak' identity which is incompatible with the strong cultural attachments required by a 'politics of authenticity'. And universal values can be seen as a strong assertion of the 'ethnia of the West' (as in the later Husserl), but also as a way of fostering – at least tendentially – an attitude of respect and tolerance *vis-à-vis* cultural diversity.

It would certainly be a mistake to think that concepts such as 'universal' and 'particular' have exactly the same meaning in both debates; but it would also be mistaken to assume that the continuous interaction of both debates has had no effect on the central categories of each. This interaction has given way to ambiguities and displacements of meaning which are – I think – the source of a certain political productivity. It is to these displacements and interactions that I want to refer in this essay. My question, put in its simplest terms, is the following: what happens with the categories of 'universal' and 'particular' once they become tools in the language games that shape contemporary politics? What is performed through them? What displacements of meaning are at the root of their current political productivity?

Multiculturalism

Let us take both debates successively and see the points in which each cuts across the central categories of the other. Multiculturalism first. The question can be formulated in these terms: is a pure culture of difference possible, a pure particularism which does away entirely with any kind of universal principle? There are various reasons to doubt that this is possible. In the first place, to assert a purely separate and differential identity is to assert that this identity is constituted *through* cultural pluralism and difference. There is no way that a particular group living in a wider community can live a monadic existence – on the contrary, part of the definition of its own identity is the construction of a complex and elaborated system of relations with other groups. And these relations will have to be regulated by norms and principles which transcend the particularism of *any* group. To assert, for instance, the right of all ethnic groups to cultural autonomy is to make an argumentative claim which can only be justified on universal grounds. The assertion of one's own particularity requires the appeal of something transcending it. The more particular a group is, the less it will be able to control the global communitarian terrain within which it operates, and the more universally grounded will have to be the justification of its claims.

But there is another reason why a politics of pure difference would be self-defeating. To assert one's own *differential* identity involves, as we have just argued, the inclusion in that identity of the other, as that from whom one delimits oneself. But it is easy to see that a fully achieved differential identity would involve the sanctioning of the existing *status quo* in the relation between groups. For an identity which is purely differential *vis-à-vis* other groups has to assert the identity of the other at the same time as its own and, as a result, cannot have identity claims in relation to those other groups. Let us suppose that a group *has* such claims – for instance, the demand for equal opportunities in employment and education, or even the right to have confessional schools. In so far as these are claims presented as rights that I share as a member of the community with all other groups, they presuppose that I am not simply different from the others but, in some fundamental respects, equal to them. If it is asserted that all particular groups have the right to respect of their own particularity, this means that they are equal to each other in some ways. Only in a situation in which all groups were different from each other, and in which none of them wanted to be anything other than what they are, would the pure logic of difference exclusively govern the relations between groups. In all other scenarios the logic of difference will be interrupted by a logic of equivalence and equality. It is not for nothing that a pure logic of difference – the notion of separate developments – lies at the root of apartheid.

This is the reason why the struggle of *any* group that attempts to assert its own identity against a hostile environment is always confronted by two opposite but symmetrical dangers for which there is no logical solution, no square circle – only precarious and contingent attempts of mediation. If the group tries to assert its identity *as it is at that moment*, as its location within the community at large is defined by the system of exclusions dictated by the dominant groups, it condemns itself to a perpetually marginalized and ghettoized existence. Its cultural values can be easily retrieved as 'folklore' by the establishment. If, on the other hand, it struggles to change its location within the community and to break with its situation of marginalization, it has to engage in a plurality of political initiatives which take it beyond the limits defining its present identity – for instance, struggles within the existing institutions. As these institutions are, however, ideologically and culturally moulded by the dominant groups, the danger is that the differential identity of the struggling group will be lost. Whether the new groups will manage to transform the institutions, or whether the logic of the institutions will manage to dilute – via co-option – the identity of those groups is something which, of course, cannot be decided beforehand and depends on a hegemonic struggle. But what is certain is that there is no major historical change in which the identity of *all* intervening forces is not transformed. There is no possibility of victory in terms of an *already acquired* cultural authenticity. The increasing awareness of this fact explains the centrality of the concept of 'hybridization' in contemporary debates.

If we look for an example of the early emergence of this alternative in European history, we can refer to the opposition between social-democrats and revolutionary syndicalists in the decades preceding the First World War. The classical Marxist solution to the problem of the disadjustment between the particularism of the working class and the universality of the task of socialist transformation had been the assumption of an increasing simplification of the social structure under capitalism: as a result, the working class as a homogeneous subject would embrace the vast majority of the population and could take up the task of universal transformation. With this type of prognostic discredited at the turn of the century, two possible solutions remained open: either to accept a dispersion of democratic struggles only loosely unified by a semi-corporative working class, or to foster a politics of pure identity by a working class unified through revolutionary violence. The first road led to what has been depicted as social-democratic integration: the working class was co-opted by a State in whose management it participated but whose mechanisms it could not master. The second road led to working-class segregationism through violence and the rejection of all participation in democratic institutions. It is important to realize that the myth of the general strike in Sorel was not a device to keep a purely working-class identity as a condition for a revolutionary victory. As the revolutionary strike was a regulative idea rather than an actual possible event, it was not a real strategy for the seizure of power: its function was exhausted in being a mechanism endlessly recreating the workers' separate identity. In the option between a politics of identity and the transformation of the relations of force between groups, Sorelianism can be seen as an extreme form of unilateralization of the first alternative.

If, however, we renounce a unilateral solution, then the tension between these two contradictory extremes cannot be eradicated: it is there to stay, and a strategic calculation can only consist of the pragmatic negotiations between them. Hybridization is not a marginal phenomenon but the very terrain in which contemporary political identities are constructed. Let us just consider a formula such as 'strategic essentialism' which has been much used lately.

For a variety of reasons, I am not entirely satisfied with it, but it has the advantage of bringing to the fore the antinomic alternatives to which we have been referring and the need for a politically negotiated equilibrium between them. 'Essentialism' alludes to a strong identity politics, without which there can be no bases for political calculation and action. But that essentialism is only strategic – that is it points, at the very moment of its constitution, to its own contingency and its own limits.

This contingency is central to understanding what is perhaps the most prominent feature of contemporary politics: the full recognition of the limited and fragmented character of its historical agents. Modernity started with the aspiration to a limitless historical actor, who would be able to ensure the fullness of a perfectly instituted social order. Whatever the road leading to that fullness – an 'invisible hand' which would hold together a multiplicity of disperse individual wills, or a universal class who would ensure a transparent and rational system of social relations – it always implied that the agents of that historical transformation would be able to overcome all particularism and all limitation and bring about a society reconciled with itself. That is what, for modernity, true universality meant. The starting point of contemporary social and political struggles is, on the contrary, the strong assertion of their particularity, the conviction that none of them is capable, on its own, of bringing about the fullness of the community. But precisely because of that, as we have seen, this particularity cannot be constructed through a pure 'politics of difference' but has to appeal, as the very condition of its own assertion, to universal principles. The question that at this point arises is to what extent this universality is the same as the universality of modernity, to what extent the very idea of a fullness of society experiences, in this changed political and intellectual climate, a radical mutation that – while maintaining the double reference to the universal and the particular – entirely transforms the logic of their articulation. Before answering this question, however, we have to move to our second debate, that related to the critique of foundationalism.

Contexts and the Critique of Foundationalism

Let us start our discussion with a very common proposition: that there is no truth or value independent of the context, that the validity of any statement is only contextually determined. In one sense, of course, this proposition is uncontroversial and a necessary corollary of the critique of foundationalism. To pass from it to assert the incommensurability of contexts and to draw from there an argument in defense of cultural pluralism seems to be only a logical move, and I am certainly not prepared to argue otherwise. There is, however, one difficulty that this whole reasoning does not contemplate, and it is the following: how to determine the limits of a context. Let us accept that all identity is a differential identity. In that case two consequences follow: (1) that, as in a Saussurean *system,* each identity is what it is only through its differences from all the others; (2) that the context has to be a closed one – if all identities depend on the differential *system*, unless the latter defines its own limits, no identity would be finally constituted. But nothing is more difficult – from a logical point of view – than defining those limits. If we had a foundational perspective we could appeal to an ultimate ground which would be the source of all differences; but if we are dealing with a true pluralism of differences, if the differences are *constitutive*, we cannot go, in the search for the systematic limits that define a context, beyond the differences themselves. Now, the only way of defining a context is, as we have said, through its limits, and the only way of defining those limits is to point out what is beyond them. But what is beyond the limits can only be other differences, and in that case – given the constitutive character of all differences – it is impossible to establish whether these new differences are internal or external to the context. The very possibility of a limit and, *ergo*, a context, is thus jeopardized.

As I have argued elsewhere (see chapter 3), the only way out of this difficulty is to postulate a beyond which is not one more difference but something which poses a threat to (that is negates) all the differences within that context – or, better, that the context constitutes itself as such through the act of exclusion of something alien, of a radical otherness. Now, this possibility has three consequences which are capital for our argument:

1. The first is that antagonism and exclusion are constitutive of all identity. Without limits through which a (non-dialectical) negativity is constructed, we would have an indefinite dispersion of differences whose absence of systematic limits would make any differential identity impossible. But this very function of constituting differential identities through antagonistic limits is

what, at the same time, destabilizes and subverts those differences. For if the limit poses an equal threat to all the differences, it makes them all equivalent to each other, interchangeable with each other as far as the limit is concerned. This already announces the possibility of a relative universalization through equivalential logics, which is not incompatible with a differential particularism, but is required by the very logic of the latter.

2. The system is what is required for the differential identities to be constituted, but the only thing – exclusion – which can constitute the system and thus make possible those identities, is also what subverts them. (In deconstructive terms: the conditions of possibility of the system are also its conditions of impossibility.) Contexts have to be internally subverted in order to become possible. The system (as in Jacques Lacan's object *petit a*) is that which the very logic of the context requires but which is, however, impossible. It is present, if you want, through its absence. But this means two things. First, that all differential identity will be constitutively split; it will be the crossing point between the logic of difference and the logic of equivalence. This introduces into it a radical undecidability. Second, that although the fullness and universality of society is unachievable, its need does not disappear: it will always show itself through the presence of its absence. Again, what we see announcing itself here is an intimate connection between the universal and the particular which does not consist, however, in the subsumption of the latter in the former.

3. Finally, if that impossible object – the system – cannot be represented but needs, however, to show itself within the field of representation, the means of that representation will be constitutively inadequate. Only the particulars are such means. As a result the systematicity of the system, the moment of its impossible totalization, will be symbolized by particulars which contingently assume such a representative function. This means, first, that the particularity of the particular is subverted by this function of representing the universal, but second, that a certain particular, by making its own particularity the signifying body of a universal representation, comes to occupy – within the system of differences as a whole – a hegemonic role. This anticipates our main conclusion: in a society (and this is finally the case of *any* society) in which its fullness – the moment of its universality – is unachievable, the relation between the universal and the particular is a hegemonic relation.

Let us see in more detail the logic of that relation. I will take as an example the 'universalization' of the popular symbols of Perónism in the Argentina of the 1960s and 1970s. After the coup of 1955 which overthrew the Perónist regime, Argentina entered a period of institutional instability which lasted for over twenty years. Perónism and other popular organizations were proscribed, and the succession of military governments and fraudulent civilian regimes which occupied the government were clearly incapable of meeting the popular demands of the masses through the existing institutional channels. So, there was a succession of less and less representative regimes and an accumulation of unfulfilled democratic demands. These demands were certainly particular ones and came from very different groups. The fact that all of them were rejected by the dominant regimes established an increasing relation of equivalence between them. This equivalence, it is important to realize, did not express any essential a priori unity. On the contrary, its only ground was the rejection of all those demands by successive regimes. In terms of our previous terminology, their unification within a context or system of differences was the pure result of all of them being antagonized by the dominant sectors.

Now, as we have seen, this contextual unification of a system of differences can only take place at the price of weakening the purely differential identities, through the operation of a logic of equivalence which introduces a dimension of relative universality. In our example, people felt that through the differential particularity of their demands – housing, union rights, level of wages, protection of national industry, etcetera – something equally present in all of them was expressed, which was opposition to the regime. It is important to realize that this dimension of universality was not at odds with the particularism of the demands – or even of the groups entering into the equivalential relation – but grew out of it. A certain more universal perspective, which developed out of the inscription of particular demands in a wider popular language of resistance, was the result of the expansion of the equivalential logic. A pure particularism of the demands of the groups, which had entirely avoided the equivalential logic, would have been possible only if the regime had succeeded in dealing separately with the particular demands and had absorbed them in a 'transformistic' way. But in any process of hegemonic decline, this transformistic absorption becomes impossible and the equivalential logics interrupt the pure particularism of the individual democratic demands.

As we can see, this dimension of universality reached through equivalence is very different from the universality which results from an underlying essence or an unconditioned a priori principle. It is not a regulative idea either – empirically unreachable but with an unequivocal teleological content – because it cannot exist apart from the system of equivalences from which it proceeds. But this has important consequences for both the content and the function of that universality. We have seen before that the moment of totalization or universalization of the community – the moment of its fullness – is an impossible object which can only acquire a discursive presence through a particular content which divests itself of its particularity in order to represent that fullness. To return to our Argentinian example, this was precisely the role that, in the 1960s and 1970s, was played by the popular symbols of Perónism. As I said earlier, the country had entered into a rapid process of de-institution-alization, so the equivalential logics could operate freely. The Perónist movement itself lacked a real organization and was rather a series of symbols and a loose language unifying a variety of political initiatives. Finally, Perón himself was in exile in Madrid, intervening only in a distant way in his movement's actions, being very careful not to take any definitive stand in the factional struggles within Perónism. In those circumstances, he was in ideal conditions to become the 'empty signifier' incarnating the moment of universality in the chain of equivalences which unified the popular camp. And the ulterior destiny of Perónism in the 1970s clearly illustrates the essential ambiguity inherent in any hegemonic process: on the one hand, the fact that the symbols of a particular group at some point assume a function of universal representation certainly gives a hegemonic power to that group; but, on the other hand, the fact that this function of universal representation has been acquired at the price of weakening the differential particularism of the original identity, leads necessarily to the conclusion that this hegemony is going to be precarious and threatened. The wild logic of emptying the signifiers of universality through the expansion of the equivalential chains means that no fixing and particular limitation on the sliding of the signified under the signifier is going to be permanently assured. This is what happened to Perónism after the electoral victory of 1973 and Perón's return to Argentina. Perón was no longer an empty signifier but the president of the country, who had to carry out concrete politics. Yet the chains of equivalences constructed by the different factions of his movements had gone beyond any possibility of control – even by Perón himself. The result was the bloody process which led to the military dictatorship in 1976.

The Dialectics of Universality

The previous developments lead us to the following conclusion: the dimension of universality – resulting from the incompletion of all differential identities – cannot be eliminated so long as a community is not entirely homogeneous (if it *were* homogeneous, what would disappear is not only universality but also the very distinction universality/particularity). This dimension is, however, just an empty place unifying a set of equivalential demands. We have to determine the nature of this place both in terms of its contents and of its function. As far as the content is concerned, it does not have one of its own but just that which is given to it by a transient articulation of equivalential demands. There is a paradox implicit in the formulation of universal principles, which is that all of them have to present themselves as valid without exception, while, even in its own terms, this universality can easily be questioned and can never be actually maintained. Let us take a universal principle such as the right of nations to self-determination. As a universal right, it claims to be valid in any circumstance. Let us suppose now that within a nation genocidal practices are taking place: in that case has the international community the duty to intervene, or is the principle of self-determination an unconditionally valid one? The paradox is that while the principle has to be formulated as universally valid, there will always be exceptions to that universal validity. But perhaps the paradox proceeds from believing that this universality has a content of its own, whose logical implications can be analytically deduced, without realizing that its own function – within a particular language game – is to make discursively possible a chain of equivalential effects, but without pretending that this universality can operate beyond the context of its emergence. There are innumerable contexts in which the principle of national self-determination is a perfectly valid way of totalizing and universalizing a historical experience.

But in that case, if we always know beforehand that no

56

universalization will live up to its task, if it will always fail to deliver the goods, why does the equivalential aggregation have to express itself through the universal? The answer is to be found in what we said before about the formal structure on which the aggregation depends. The 'something identical' shared by all the terms of the equivalential chain – that which makes the equivalence possible – cannot be something positive (that is one more difference which could be defined in its particularity), but proceeds from the unifying effects that the external threat poses to an otherwise perfectly heterogeneous set of differences (particularities). The 'something identical' can only be the pure, abstract, absent fullness of the community, which lacks, as we have seen, any direct form of representation and expresses itself through the equivalence of the differential terms. But, in that case, it is essential that the chain of equivalences remains open: otherwise its closure could only be the result of one more difference specifiable in its particularity and we would not be confronted with the fullness of the community as an absence. The open character of the chain means that what is expressed through it has to be universal and not particular. Now, this universality needs – for its expression – to be incarnated in something essentially incommensurable with it: a particularity (as in our example of the right to self-determination). This is the source of the tension and ambiguities surrounding all these so-called 'universal' principles: all of them *have* to be formulated as limitless principles, expressing a universality transcending them: but they all, for essential reasons, sooner or later become entangled in their own contextual particularism and are incapable of fulfilling their universal function.

As far as the function (as different from the content) of the 'universal' is concerned, we have said enough to make clear what it consists of: it is exhausted in introducing chains of equivalence in an otherwise purely differential world. This is the moment of hegemonic aggregation and articulation and can operate in two ways. The first is to inscribe particular identities and demands as links in a wider chain of equivalences, thereby giving each of them a 'relative' universalization. If, for instance, feminist demands enter into chains of equivalence with those of black groups, ethnic minorities, civil rights activists, etcetera, they acquire a more global perspective than is the case where they remain restricted to their own particularism. The second is to give a particular demand a function of universal representation – that is to give it the value of a horizon giving coherence to the chain of equivalences and, at the same time, keeping it indefinitely open. To give just a few examples: the socialization of the means of production was not considered as a narrow demand concerning the economy but as the 'name' for a wide variety of equivalential effects radiating over the whole society. The introduction of a market economy played a similar role in Eastern Europe after 1989. The return of Perón, in our Argentinian example, was also conceived in the early 1970s as the prelude to a much wider historical transformation. Which particular demand, or set of demands, are going to play this function of universal representation is something which cannot be determined by a priori reasons (if we could do so, this would mean that there is something in the particularity of the demand which predetermined it to fulfil that role, and that would be in contradiction to our whole argument).

We can now return to the two debates which were the starting point of our reflection. As we can see, there are several points in which they interact and in which parallelism can be detected. We have said enough about multiculturalism for our argument concerning the limits of particularism to be clear. A *pure* particularistic stand is self-defeating because it has to provide a ground for the constitution of the differences *as* differences, and such a ground can only be a new version of an essentialist universalism. (If we have a *system* of differences A/B/C, etcetera, we have to account for this systemic dimension and that leads us straight into the discourse of ground. If we have a plurality of *separate* elements A, B, C, etcetera, which do not constitute a system, we still have to account for this separation – to be separated is also a form of relation between objects – and we are again entangled, as Leibnitz knew well, in the positing of a ground. The pre-established harmony of the monads is as essential a ground as the Spinozean totality.) So, the only way out of this dilemma is to maintain the dimension of universality but to propose a different form for its articulation with the particular. This is what we have tried to provide in the preceding pages through the notion of the universal as an empty but ineradicable place.

It is important, however, to realize that this type of articulation would be theoretically unthinkable if we did not introduce into the picture some of the central tenets of the contemporary critique of foundationalism (it would be unthinkable, for instance, in a Habermasian perspective). If meaning is fixed beforehand either, in a strong sense, by a radical ground (a position that fewer and fewer people would sustain today) or, in a weaker version, through the regulative principle of an undistorted communication, the very possibility of the ground as an empty place which is politically and contingently filled by a variety of social forces disappears. Differences would not be constitutive because something previous to their play *already* fixes the limit of their possible variation and establishes an external tribunal to *judge* them. Only the critique of a universality which is determined in all its essential dimensions by the metaphysics of presence opens the way for a *theoretical* apprehension of the notion of 'articulation' that we are trying to elaborate – as different from a purely impressionistic apprehension, in terms of a discourse structured through concepts which are perfectly incompatible with it. (We always have to remember Pascal's critique of those who think that they are already converted because they have just started thinking of getting converted.)

But if the debate concerning multiculturalism can draw clear advantages from the contemporary critique of foundationalism (broadly speaking, the whole range of intellectual developments embraced by labels such as 'postmodernism' and 'post-structuralism'), these advantages also work in the opposite direction. For the requirements of a politics based on a universality compatible with an increasing expansion of cultural differences are clearly incompatible with some versions of postmodernism – particularly those which conclude from the critique of foundationalism that there is an implosion of all meaning and the entry into a world of 'simulation' (Baudrillard). I don't think that this is a conclusion which follows at all. As we have argued, the impossibility of a universal ground does not eliminate its need: it just transforms the ground into an empty place which can be partially filled in a variety of ways (the strategies of this filling is what politics is about). Let us go back for a moment to the question of contextualization. If we could have a 'saturated' context we would indeed be confronted with a plurality of incommensurable spaces without any possible tribunal deciding between them. But, as we have seen, any such saturated context is impossible. Yet,the conclusion which follows from this verification is not that there is a formless dispersion of meaning without even any possible kind of relative articulation but, rather, that whatever plays such an articulating role is not predetermined to it by the form of the dispersion as such. This means first that all articulation is contingent and, second, that the articulating moment as such is always going to be an empty place

– the various attempts at filling it being transient and submitted to contestation. As a result, at any historical moment, whatever dispersion of differences exists in society is going to be submitted to contradictory processes of contextualization and de-contextualization. For instance, those discourses attempting to close a context around certain principles or values will be confronted and limited by discourses of *rights*, which try to limit the closure of any context. This is what makes so unconvincing the attempts by contemporary neo-Aristotelians such as McIntyre at accepting only the contextualizing dimension and closing society around a substantive vision of the common good. Contemporary social and political struggles open, I think, strategies of filling the empty place of the common good. The ontological implications of the thought accompanying these 'filling' strategies clarifies, in turn, the horizon of possibilities opened by the anti-foundationalist critique. It is to these strategic logics that I want to devote the rest of this essay.

Ruling and Universality: Four Moments

We can start with some conclusions which could easily be derived from our previous analysis concerning the status of the universal. The first is that if the place of the universal is an empty one and there is no a priori reason for it not to be filled by *any* content, if the forces which fill that place are constitutively split between the concrete politics that they advocate and the ability of those politics to fill the empty place, the political language of any society whose degree of institutionalization has, to some extent, been shaken or undermined, will also be split. Let us just take a term such as 'order' (social order). What are the conditions of its universalization? Simply, that the experience of a radical disorder makes *any* order preferable to the continuity of disorder. The experience of a lack, of an absence of fullness in social relations, transforms 'order' into the signifier of an absent fullness. This explains the split we were referring to: any concrete politics, if it is capable of bringing about social order, will be judged not only according to its merits in the abstract, independently of any circumstance, but mainly in terms of that ability to bring about 'order' – a name for the absent fullness of society. ('Change', 'revolution', 'unity of the people', etcetera are other signifiers which have historically played the same role.) Since, for essential reasons as we have pointed out, the fullness of society is unreachable, this split in the identity of political agents is an absolutely constitutive 'ontological difference' – in a sense not entirely unrelated to Heidegger's use of this expression. The universal is certainly empty, and can only be filled in different contexts by concrete particulars. But, at the same time, it is absolutely essential for any kind of *political* interaction, for if the latter took place without universal reference, there would be no political interaction at all: we would only have either a complementarity of differences which would be totally non-antagonistic, or a totally antagonistic one, one where differences entirely lack any commensurability, and whose only possible resolution is the mutual destruction of the adversaries.

Now, it is our contention that politico-philosophical reflection since the ancient world has been largely conscious of this constitutive split, and has tried to provide various ways of dealing with it. These ways follow one or the other of the logical possibilities pointed out in the previous analysis. To suggest how this took place, we will briefly refer to four moments in the politico-philosophical tradition of the West in which images of the ruler have emerged which combine universality and particularity in different ways. We will refer successively to Plato's philosopher-king, to Hobbes's sovereign, to Hegel's hereditary monarch, and to Gramsci's hegemonic class.

In Plato the situation is unambiguous. There is no possible tension or antagonism between the universal and the particular. Far from being an empty place, the universal is the location of all possible meaning, and it absorbs the particular within itself. Now, for him however, there is only *one* articulation of the particularities which actualize the essential form of the community. The universal is not 'filled' from outside, but is the fullness of its own origin and expresses itself in all aspects of social organization. There can be no 'ontological difference' here between the fullness of the community and its actual political and social arrangements. Only *one* kind of social arrangement, which extends itself to the most minute aspects of social life, is compatible with what the community in its last instance is. Other forms of social organization can, of course, factually exist, but they do not have the status of alternative forms among which one has to choose according to the circumstances. They are just degenerate forms, pure corruption of being, derived from obfuscation of the mind. In so far as there is true knowledge, only one particular form of social organization realizes the universal. And if ruling is a matter of knowledge and not of prudence, only the bearer of that knowledge, the philosopher, has the right to rule. *Ergo*: a philosopher-king.

With Hobbes we are apparently at the antipodes of Plato. Far from being the sovereign, the one who has the knowledge of what the community is before any political decision, his decisions are the only source of social order. Hobbes is well aware of what we have called the 'ontological difference'. Inasmuch as the anarchy of the state of nature threatens society with radical disorder, the unification of the will of the community in the will of the ruler (or rather, the will of the ruler as the only unified will that the community can have) will count in so far as it imposes order, whatever the contents of the latter could be. Any order will be better than radical disorder. There is something close to a complete indifference here to the *content* of the social order imposed by the ruler, and an exclusive concentration on the *function* of the latter: ensuring order as such. 'Order' certainly becomes an empty place, but there is in Hobbes no hegemonic theory about the transient forms of its filling: the sovereign, the 'mortall God', fills the empty place once and forever.

So, Plato and Hobbes are apparently at the antipodes of the theoretical spectrum. For Plato, the universal is the *only* full place; for Hobbes, it is an absolutely empty place which has to be filled by the will of the sovereign. But if we look more closely at the matter, we will see that this difference between them is overshadowed by what they actually share, which is not to allow the particular any dynamics of its own *vis-à-vis* the full/empty place of the universal. In the first case, the particular has to actualize in its own body a universality transcending it; in the second case equally, although by artificial means, a particular has detached itself from the realm of particularities and has become the unchallengeable law of the community.

For Hegel, the problem is posed in different terms. Since, for him, the particularism of each stage of social organization is *aufgehoben* at a higher level, the problem of the incommensurability between particular content and universal function cannot actually arise. But the problem of the empty place emerges in relation to the moment in which the community has to *signify* itself as a totality – that is the moment of its *individuality*. This signification is obtained, as we know, through the constitutional monarch, whose physical body represents a rational totality absolutely dissimilar to that body. (This representation, in Hegel, of something which has no content of its own through something else which is its exact reverse, has very often been stressed by Slavoj Žižek, who has contributed several other examples such as the assertion, in the *Phenomenology of Spirit,* that 'the Spirit is a bone'.) But this relation, by which a physical content can represent, in its pure alienation of any spiritual content, this last content, entirely depends on the commmunity having reached, through successive sublations of its partial contents, the highest form of rationality achievable in its own sphere. For such a fully rational community no *content* can be added and it only remains, as a requirement for its completion, *the signification of the achievement of that functional rationality.* Because of that, the rational monarch cannot be an elected monarch: he has to be a hereditary one. If he were elected, *reasons* would have to be given for that election, and this process of argumentation would mean that the rationality of society would not have been achieved independently of the monarch, and that the latter would have to play a greater role than a pure function of ceremonial representation.

Finally Gramsci. The hegemonic class can only become such by linking a particular content to a universality transcending it. If we say – as Gramsci did – that the task of the Italian working class is to fulfil the tasks of national unification that the Italian people had posed themselves since the time of Machiavelli and, in some way, to complete the historical project of the *Risorgimento*, we have a double order of reference. On the one hand, a concrete political programme – that of the workers – as different from those of other political forces; but, on the other hand, that programme – that is that set of demands and political proposals – is presented as a historical vehicle for a task transcending it: the unity of the Italian nation. Now, if this 'unity of the Italian nation' was a concrete content, specifiable in a particular context, it could not be something which extended over a period of centuries and that different historical forces could bring about. However, if this *can* happen, it is because 'unity of the Italian nation' is just the name or the symbol of a lack. Precisely because it is a *constitutive* lack, there is no content which is a priori destined to fill it, and it is open to the most diverse articulations. But this means that the 'good' articulation, the one that would finally suture the link between universal task and concrete historical forces will never be found, and that all partial victory will always take place against the background of an ultimate and unsurpassable impossibility.

Viewed from this perspective the Gramscian project can be seen as a double displacement, *vis-à-vis* both Hegel and Hobbes. In one sense it is more Hobbesian than Hegelian, because, as society and State are less self-structured than in Hegel, they require a dimension of political constitution in which the representation of the unity of the community is not separated from its construction. There is a remainder of particularity which cannot be eliminated from the representation of that unity (unity = individuality in the Hegelian sense). The presence of this remainder is what is specific to the hegemonic relation. The hegemonic class is somewhere in between the Hegelian monarch and the Leviathan. But it can equally be said that Gramsci is more Hegelian than Hobbesian, in the sense that the political moment in his analysis presupposes an image of social crises which is far less radical than in Hobbes. Gramsci's 'organic crises' fall far short, in terms of their degrees of social structuring, from the Hobbesian state of nature. In some senses, the succession of hegemonic regimes can be seen as a series of 'partial covenants' – partial because, as society is more structured than in Hobbes, people have more conditions under which to enter into the political covenant: but partial also because, as the result of that, they also have more reasons to substitute the sovereign.

These last points allow us to go back to our earlier discussion concerning contemporary particularistic struggles and to inscribe it within the politico-philosophical tradition. In the same way that we have presented Gramsci's problematic through the displacements that he introduces *vis-à-vis* the two approaches that we have symbolized in Hobbes and Hegel, we could present the political alternatives open to multicultural struggles through similar displacements *vis-à-vis* Gramsci's approach. The first and most obvious displacement is to conceive a society which is more particularistic and fragmented and less amenable than Gramsci's to enter into unified hegemonic articulations. The second is that the loci from which the articulation takes place – for Gramsci they were locations such as the Party, or the State (in an expanded sense) – are also going to be more plural and less likely to generate a chain of totalizing effects. What we have called the remainder of particularism inherent in any hegemonic centrality grows thicker but also more plural. Now, this has mixed effects from the viewpoint of a democratic politics. Let us imagine a Jacobinic scenario. The public sphere is one, the place of power is one but is empty, and a plurality of political forces can occupy the latter. In one sense we can say that this is an ideal situation for democracy, because the place of power is empty and we can conceive the democratic process as a partial articulation of the empty universality of the community and the particularism of the transient political forces incarnating it. This is true, but precisely because the universal place is empty, it can be occupied by any force, not necessarily democratic. As is well known, this is one of the roots of contemporary totalitarianism (Lefort).

If, on the contrary, the place of power is not unique, the remainder, as we said, will be weightier, and the possibility of constructing a common public sphere through a series of equivalential effects cutting across communities will clearly be less. This has ambiguous results. On the one hand, communities are certainly more protected in the sense that a Jacobinic totalitarianism is less likely. But, on the other hand, for reasons that have been pointed out earlier, this also favours the maintenance of the *status quo*. We can perfectly well imagine a modified Hobbesian scenario in which the law respects communities – no longer individuals – in their private sphere, while the main decisions concerning the future of the community as a whole are the preserve of a neo-Leviathan – for instance a quasi-omnipotent technocracy. To realize that this is not at all an unrealistic scenario, we only have to think of Samuel Huntington and, more generally, of contemporary corporatist approaches.

The other alternative is more complex but it is the only one, I think, compatible with a true democratic politics. It wholly accepts the plural and fragmented nature of contemporary societies but, instead of remaining in this particularistic moment, it tries to inscribe this plurality in equivalential logics which make possible the construction of new public spheres. Difference and particularisms are the necessary starting point, but out of it, it is possible to open the way to a relative universalization of values which can be the basis for a popular hegemony. This universalization and its open character certainly condemns all identity to an unavoidable hybridization, but hybridization does not necessarily mean decline through the loss of identity: it can also mean empowering existing identities through the opening of new possibilities. Only a conservative identity, closed on itself, could experience hybridization as a loss. But this democratico-hegemonic possibility has to recognize the constitutive contextualized/decontextualized terrain of its constitution and take full advantage of the political possibilities that this undecidability opens.

All this finally amounts to saying is that the particular can only fully realize itself if it constantly keeps open, and constantly re-defines, its relation to the universal.

5

'The Time is Out of Joint'

> Since this singular end of the political would correspond to the presentation of an absolute living reality, this is one more reason to think that the essence of the political will always have the inessential figure, the very anessence of a ghost.
>
> Jacques Derrida, *Spectres of Marx*

Halfway through *Spectres of Marx* (SM), Derrida links the concept of production to that of trauma and speaks of 'the spectral spiritualization that is at work in any *tekhne*' (*SM*, p. 97). He immediately connects this assertion to Freud's remarks concerning the three traumas inflicted on the narcissism of the decentred man: the psychological trauma derived from the psychoanalytic discovery of the unconscious, the biological trauma resulting from the Darwinian findings about human descent, and the cosmological trauma proceeding from the Copernican revolution. To this Derrida adds the decentring effects coming from Marxism which, according to him, accumulate and put the other three together:

> The century of 'Marxism' will have been that of the techno-scientific and effective decentring of the earth, of geopolitics, of the *anthropos* in its onto-theological identity or its genetic properties, of the *ego cogito* – and of the very concept of narcissism whose aporias are, let us say in order to go too quickly and save ourselves a lot of references, the explicit theme of deconstruction. (*SM*, p.98)

So deconstruction inscribes itself in a secular movement of decentring, to which Marxism itself belongs. In fact, at various points of *Spectres of Marx*, Derrida insists that deconstruction would be either inconceivable or irrelevant if it were not related to the spirit or the tradition of a certain Marxism. And yet deconstruction is not *just* Marxism: it is a certain operation practised in the body of Marxism, the locating in Marx's texts of an area of undecidability which, in Derrida's terms, is that circumscribed by the opposition between *spirit* and *spectre*, between *ontology* and *hauntology*. The performing of this deconstructive operation – to which the last two chapters of the book are devoted – is far from a purely academic exercise: the very possibility of justice – but also of politics – is at stake. Without the constitutive dislocation that inhabits all hauntology – and that ontology tries to conceal – there would be no politics, just a programmed, predetermined reduction of the other to the same:

> It is easy to go from disadjusted to unjust. That is our problem: how to justify this passage from disadjustment (with its rather more techno-ontological value affecting a presence) to an injustice that would no longer be ontological? And what if disadjustment were on the contrary the condition of justice? And what if this double register condensed its enigma, precisely (*justement*), and potentialized its superpower in that which gives its unheard-of force to Hamlet's words: 'The time is out of joint'? (*SM*, pp. 19–20)

To find a double logic in Marx's work, to detect in the Marxian texts a double gesture that the theory makes possible but is unable to control conceptually in a credible synthesis: all this looks rather familiar. Since the end of the nineteenth century, this duality, deeply inscribed in Marx's work, has been the object of countless analyses. The duality of, or the oppositions between, economic determinism and the ethical orientation of socialism, between economism and the primacy of politics, even between the 'scientific' and the 'ideological' components of the theory, have been not only recurrent themes in Marxist discussions but the very issues that have made possible a history of Marxism. However, none of these apparent reformulations of the terms of a widely perceived dualism has been similar to the others. We are not dealing with a purely nominalistic operation of renaming: the displacement that these reformulations operate, the logics of the social they imply, and, above all, the political strategies they make possible are radically different.

Derrida does not trace the genealogy of his intervention in the Marxist text. This is regrettable, among other things because the specificity, originality and potentialities of his intervention do not come sufficiently to light. In what follows, I will try to stress some of these specific features, as well as their originality *vis-à-vis* other comparable attempts. To this end, I will refer to what I think are the two central theoretical points in Derrida's book: the logic of the spectre (the hauntology) and the category of messianism.

The Logic of the Spectre

[T]he spectre is a paradoxical incorporation, the becoming-body, a certain phenomenal and carnal form of the spirit. It becomes, rather, some 'thing' that remains difficult to name: neither soul nor body, and both one and the other. For it is flesh and phenomenality that give to the spirit its spectral apparition, but which disappear right away in the apparition, in the very coming of the *revenant* or the return of the spectre. There is something disappeared, departed in the apparition itself as reapparition of the departed. (SM, p. 6)

Anachronism is essential to spectrality: the spectre, interrupting all specularity, desynchronizes time. The very essence of spectrality is to be found in this undecidability between flesh and spirit: it is not purely body – for, in that case, there would be no spectrality at all; but it is not pure spirit either – for the passage through the flesh is crucial:

For there is no ghost, there is never any becoming-spectre of the spirit without at least an appearance of flesh, in a space of invisible visibility, like the disappearing of an apparition. For there to be ghost, there must be a return to the body, but to a body that is more abstract than ever. The spectrogenic process corresponds therefore to a paradoxical *incorporation*. Once ideas or thoughts (*Gedanke*) are detached from the substratum, one engenders some ghost by *giving them a body*.

(SM, p. 126)

From this point onward, Derrida makes a classic deconstructive move: the spectre being undecidable between the two extremes of body and spirit, these extremes themselves become contaminated by that undecidability. Thus, having shown how, in Marx's analysis of commodity, exchange value depends for its constitution on a spectral logic, Derrida concludes that this logic is not absent from use value either:

The said use-value of the said ordinary sensuous thing, simply *hule*, the wood of the wooden table concerning which Marx supposes that it has not yet begun to 'dance', its very form, the form that informs its *hule*, must indeed have at least promised it to iterability, to substitution, to exchange, to value; it must have made a start, however minimal it may have been, on an idealization that permits one to identify it as the same throughout possible repetitions, and so forth. Just as there is no pure use, there is no use-value which the possibility of exchange and commerce... has not in advance inscribed in an *out-of-use* – an excessive signification that cannot be reduced to the useless.

(*SM*, p. 160)

Similarly, if the spirit is something whose invisibility has to produce its own visibility, if the very constitution of spirit requires the visibility of the invisible, nothing is more difficult than to keep a strict separation between spirit and spectre. Once this point has been reached, the conclusions quickly follow. We find in Marx a hauntology, an argument about spectrality at the very heart of the constitution of the social link. Time being 'out of joint', dislocation corrupting the identity with itself of any present, we have a constitutive anachronism that is at the root of any identity. Any 'life' emerges out of a more basic life/death dichotomy – it is not 'life' as uncontaminated presence but *survie* that is the condition of any presence. Marx, however, attempted the critique of the hauntological from the perspective of an ontology. If the spectre inhabits the root of the social link in bourgeois society, the transcendence of the latter, the arrival at a time that is no longer 'out of joint', the realization of a society fully reconciled with itself will open the way to the 'end of ideology' – that is to a purely 'ontological' society which, after the consummation of the proletarian millennium, will look to hauntology as its past. And since hauntology is inherent to politics, the transcendence of the split between being and appearance will mean the end of politics. (We could, in fact, put the argument in Saint-Simonian terms: the transition from the government of men to the administration of things.) If, however, as the deconstructive reading shows, 'ontology' – full reconciliation – is not achievable, time is constitutively 'out of joint', and the ghost is the condition of possibility of any present, politics too becomes constitutive of the social link. We could say of the spectre what Groucho Marx said about sex: it is going to stay with us for a while.

This contamination of presence by the spectre can be considered from the two perspectives involved in a double genitive. There are, in the first place, spectres of Marx, in so far as Marx himself – an abbreviation for communism – is haunting us today as a horizon preventing the possibility of its final exorcism by the apparently triumphant capitalist 'democracies' (here the main reference is to Fukuyama). But there are also the spectres of Marx that visited Marx himself and prevented him from establishing a non-haunted ontology. Thus, the ground we reach – that of a present never identical with itself – is the very terrain of this phantasmatic, anessential practice we call politics.

What to say about this Derridian sequence? A first remark – first both temporally and logically – is that I have nothing to object to. The deconstructive operation is impeccable, the horizons that it opens are far-reaching, and the intertextuality within which it takes place is highly illuminating. However, as with any deconstruction worthy of the name, there is a plurality of directions in which one can move, and it is to consider this plurality that I would like to pause for a moment. My own work has largely concentrated on the deconstruction of Marxist texts, and I could, *prima facie*, relate what I have called hegemonic logic[1] – which silently deconstructs Marxist categories – to the logic of the spectre as described by Derrida. Others, too, have recently linked 'deconstruction' and 'hegemony'. Simon Critchley, for instance, asserts:

> Against the troubling tendency to subordinate the political to the socio-economic within Marx's 'ontology'. . . Derrida's argument for a logic of spectrality within Marxism can be linked to the claim for the irreducibility of the political understood as that moment where the sedimented meanings of the socio-economic are contested. Following Ernesto Laclau's radicalization of Gramsci, one might link the logic of spectrality to the logic of hegemony; that is if one renounces – as one must – the communist eschatological 'a-theodicy' of the economic contradictions of capitalism inevitably culminating in revolution, then politics and politico-cultural-ideological hegemonization is indispensable to the possibility of radical change.

I hesitate, however, to entirely endorse such an apparently obvious assimilation. Although there is no incompatibility between hegemony and spectral logic as far as the latter goes, a hegemonic logic presupposes two further steps beyond spectrality that I am not sure Derrida is prepared to take:

1. Spectrality presupposes, as we have seen, an undecidable relation between spirit and flesh which contaminates, in turn, these two poles. It presupposes, in that sense, a weakened form of incarnation. Weakened because a full incarnation – an incarnation in the Christian sense – transforms the flesh into a purely transparent medium through which we can see an *entirely* spiritual reality with no connection to its incarnating body. God's mediation is what establishes the link between spirit and flesh in so far as He is at an infinite distance from both. So the lack of natural connection between both poles is what transforms the flesh into the medium through which the spirit shows itself. At the same time, however, it is this lack of connection that prevents the contamination of one by the other. No doubt this Christian polarity can be deconstructed in turn, but the point is that this deconstruction will not take place through the collapse of the frontier between spirit and spectre. For in the spectre the relation between spirit and flesh is much more intimate: there is no divine mediation that both sanctions and supersedes the essential heterogeneity of the two poles. Now, a hegemonic relation is one in which a certain body presents itself as the incarnation of a certain spirit. The hegemonic relation is certainly spectral: a certain body tries to present its particular features as the expression of something transcending its own particularity. The body is an undecidable point in which universality and particularity get confused, but the very fact that other bodies compete to be the incarnating ones, that they are alternative forms of materialization of the same 'spirit', suggests a kind of autonomization of the latter which cannot be explained solely by the pure logic of spectrality.

2. Of what does this autonomization consist? This is our second step. Let us remember that any step that is taken out of the logic of spectrality cannot be in contradiction to the latter but must, on the contrary, presuppose it. If the autonomization of the 'spirit' is to take place within spectrality, 'autonomy' cannot mean identify with oneself, self-representation, because that would precisely restore a rigid frontier between 'spirit' and 'spectre'. But autonomy does not require full identity as its precondition: it can also emerge out of a constitutive impossibility, an absolute limit whose forms of representation will be necessarily inadequate. Let us suppose a situation of

generalized social disorder: in such a situation 'order' becomes the name of an absent fullness, and if that fullness is constitutively unachievable, it cannot have any content of its own, any form of self-representation. 'Order' thus becomes autonomous *vis-à-vis* any particular order in so far as it is the name of an absent fullness that no concrete social order can achieve (the same can be said of similar terms such as 'revolution', 'unity of the people', etcetera). That fullness is present, however, as that which is absent and needs, as a result, to be represented in some way. Now, its means of representation will be constitutively inadequate, for they can only be particular contents that assume, in certain circumstances, a function of representation of the impossible universality of the community. This relation, by which a certain particular content overflows its own particularity and becomes the incarnation of the absent fullness of society is exactly what I call a hegemonic relation. As we can see, it presupposes the logic of the spectre: the fullness of the 'spirit', as it has no content of its own, can exist only through its parasitic attachment to some particular body; but that body is subverted and deformed in its own particularity as it becomes the embodiment of fullness. This means, *inter alia*, that the anachronistic language of revolutions, which Marx refers to and Derrida analyses, is inevitable: the old revolution is present in the new one, not in its particularity but in its universal function of being *a* revolution, as the incarnation of the revolutionary principle as such. And the Marxian aspiration of a revolutionary language that only expresses the present, in which the 'content' overcomes 'phraseology', is a pure impossibility. If the fullness of the revolution – as all fullness – is unachievable, we cannot but have a dissociation between the revolutionary content and the fullness of a pure revolutionary foundation, and this dissociation will reproduce *sine die* the logic of spectrality and the split between 'phraseology' and 'content'.

What precedes is an attempt to show the type of move that I would make out of the logic of spectrality. But, as I said, it is not the only move that one can make. The steps that lead from the logic of spectrality to a hegemonic logic are steps that the former logic certainly makes possible, but they are not necessary corollaries that are derived from it.

But what political consequences does Derrida himself draw from his deconstruction of Marx's texts? Although these consequences are not entirely developed in his book, we can get a broad hint of the direction that Derrida is taking if we move to our second theme: the question of the messianic.

The Question of the Messianic

Let us quote Derrida again. After having indicated that both Marxism and religion share the formal structure of a messianic eschatology, he asserts:

> While it is common to both of them, with the exception of the content . . . it is also the case that its formal structure of promise exceeds them or precedes them. Well, what remains irreducible to any deconstruction, what remains as undeconstructible as the possibility itself of deconstruction is, perhaps, a certain experience of the emancipatory promise; it is perhaps even the formality of a structural messianism, a messianism without religion, even a messianic without messianism, an idea of justice – which we distinguish from law or right and even from human rights – and an idea of democracy – which we distinguish from its current concept and from its determined predicates today. (*SM*, p. 59)

Here Derrida summarizes themes that he developed in full in 'Force of Law'. These themes and concepts require, however, that they be reinserted in the various discursive contexts within which they were originally formulated, first because these contexts considerably diverge among themselves and, second, because the high metaphoricity of some of the categories employed – such as the messianic – can lead to an undue association of these categories with the concrete historical phenomena to which they are usually applied. I cannot properly do this job in the limited space of a review, but let us, at least, make some specifications. By the 'messianic' we should not understand anything *directly* related to actual messianic movements – of the present or past – but, instead, something belonging to the general structure of experience. It is linked to the idea of 'promise'. This does not mean this or that particular promise, but the promise implicit in an originary opening to the 'other', to the unforeseeable, to the pure *event* which cannot be mastered by any aprioristic discourse. Such an event is an interruption in the normal course of things, a radical dislocation. This leads to the notion of 'justice' as linked to an absolute singularity which cannot be absorbed by the generality of law. The chasm between law and justice is one which cannot be closed. The existence of this chasm is what makes deconstruction possible. Deconstruction and justice – or, rather, deconstruction as justice – is what cannot be deconstructed. Deconstructing law – which is finally what politics is about – is possible because of this structure of experience in which the messianic, the promise and justice are categories in a relation of mutual implication.

On the basis of these premises, Derrida elaborates his concept of 'democracy to come' (*democratie à venir*). This '*à venir*' does not involve any teleological assertion – not even the limited one of a regulative idea – but simply the continual commitment to keep open the relation to the other, an opening which is always *à venir,* for the other to which one opens oneself is never already given in any aprioristic calculation. To summarize: the messianism we are speaking about is one without eschatology, without a pre-given promised land, without determinate content. It is simply the structure of promise which is inherent in all experience and whose lack of content – resulting from the radical opening to the event, to the other – is the very possibility of justice and gives its meaning only to the democracy to come. Singularity as the terrain of justice involves the radical undecidability which makes the decision possible:

> It was then a matter of thinking another historicity . . . another opening of event-ness as historicity that permitted one not to renounce, but on the contrary to open up access to an affirmative thinking of the messianic and emancipatory promise as promise: as promise and not as onto-theological or teleo-eschatological programme or design . . .
>
> But at a certain point promise and decision, which is to say responsibility, owe their possibility to the ordeal of undecidability which will always remain their condition. (*SM*, pp. 74–5)

What can we say about the various theoretical operations that Derrida performs starting from this conceptual construction? I think that we can distinguish three levels here. The first refers to the deconstruction of the concept of messianism that we have inherited from the religious but also from the Marxist tradition. This deconstruction proceeds by showing the contingent character of the articulations that have coalesced

74

around the actual historical messianisms. We can do away with the teleological and eschatological dimensions, we can even do away with all the actual contents of the historical messianisms, but what we cannot do away with is the 'promise', because it is inscribed in the structure of all experience. This, as we have seen, is not a promise of anything concrete; it is some sort of 'existential', in so far as it is what prevents any presence from being closed around itself. If we link this to the relations law/justice, undecidability/decisions, we can see the general movement of Derrida's theoretico-political intervention, which is to direct the historico-political forms back to the primary terrain of their opening to the radically heterogeneous. This is the terrain of constitutive undecidability, of an experience of the impossible that, paradoxically, makes responsibility, decision, law and – finally – the messianic itself possible in its actual historical forms. I find myself in full agreement with this movement.

Derrida's argument, however, does not stop there. From this first movement (for reasons that will become clear presently, I keep this 'from' deliberately vague, undecided between the derivative and the merely sequential), he passes to a sort of ethico-political injunction by which all the previously mentioned dimensions converge in the project of a democracy to come, which is linked to the classical notion of 'emancipation'. Derrida is very firm in his assertion that he is not at all prepared to put the latter into question. But we have to be very careful about the meaning of such a stand, because the classical notion of emancipation is no more than another name for the eschatological messianism that he is trying to deconstruct.

Various aspects have to be differentiated here. If by reasserting the classical notion of emancipation Derrida does not mean anything beyond his particular way of reasserting messianism – that is doing away with all the teleo-ontological paraphernalia of the latter and sticking to the moment of the 'promise' – then I would certainly agree with him but, in that case, the classic idea of emancipation, even if we retain from it an ultimately undeconstructible moment, is deeply transformed. I find it rather misleading to call this operation a defence of the classic notion of emancipation. But – second aspect – the classic notion of emancipation was something more than the formal structure of the promise. It was also the crystallization and synthesis of a series of contents such as the elimination of economic exploitation and all forms of discrimination, the assertion of human rights, the consolidation of civil and political freedom, and so forth. Derrida, understandably, does not want to renounce this patrimony, and it would be difficult not to join him in its defence. The difficulty, however, is that in the classic notion of emancipation the defence and grounding of all those contents were intimately connected to the teleological eschatology that Derrida is deconstructing. So, if he wants to maintain the results of his deconstruction and at the same time to defend those contents, since the ground of the latter can no longer be an eschatological articulation, there are only two ways open to him: either to show that those contents can be derived from the 'promise' as a general structure of experience, or to demonstrate that those contents are grounded in something less than such a general structure – in which case the 'promise' as such is indifferent to the actual nature of those contents.

There is, finally, a third aspect to be distinguished. The previous distinctions have to be situated against the background of the real target of Derrida's discussion in *Spectres of Marx*: the exposure of a prevalent common sense (that he exemplifies through his brilliant critique of Fukuyama) according to which the collapse of the communist regimes is supposed to mean humanity's arrival at a final stage where all human needs will be satisfied and where no messianic consummation of time is any longer to be expected. Derrida reacts against this new dominant consensus and its Hegelo-Kojèvian grounding by showing, at the empirical level, the gap between historical reality and the capitalist West's satisfied image of itself and, at the theoretical level, the inconsistencies of the notion of an end to history. It is against the background of this polemic that the whole discourse about the ever returning spectres of Marx has to be understood. What Derrida is finally saying is that isolated demands, grievances, injustices, and so forth are not empirical residues of a historical stage which has – in all essentials – been superseded, but that they are, on the contrary, the symptoms of a fundamental deadlock of contemporary societies that pushes isolated demands to some kind of phantasmatic articulation which will result in new forms of political reaggregation. The latter are not specified beyond Derrida's quick allusions to the historical limits of the 'party' form and to a 'New International' in the making. However, it is clear that any advance in formulating a theory of political reaggregation crucially depends on how the transition between the general structure of experience – the promise – and the contents of the classical emancipatory project is conceived.

This is the third level at which the argument of *Spectres of Marx* can be considered: the type of link it establishes between the promise as a (post-) transcendental or (post-) ontological (non-) ground and the ethical and political contents of an emancipatory project. This is the level at which I find the argument of *Spectres* less convincing. For here an illegitimate logical transition can easily be made. I am not necessarily asserting that Derrida is making that transition, but, at any rate, it is one frequently made by many defenders of deconstruction and one to which the very ambiguity of the Derridian texts gives some credence. The illegitimate transition is to think that from the impossibility of a presence closed in itself, from an 'ontological' condition in which the openness to the event, to the heterogeneous, to the radically other is constitutive, some kind of ethical injunction to be responsible and to keep oneself open to the heterogeneity of the other necessarily follows. This transition is illegitimate for two reasons. First, because if the promise is an 'existential' constitutive of all experience, it is always already there, before any injunction. (It is like the voluntaristic argument criticized by Ortega y Gasset: on the one hand, it asserts that life is constitutive insecurity; on the other, it launches the imperative *Vivere pericolosamente,* as if to do it or not to do it were a matter of choice.) But, second and most important, from the fact that there is the impossibility of ultimate closure and presence, it does not follow that there is an ethical imperative to 'cultivate' that openness or even less to be necessarily committed to a democratic society. I think the latter can certainly be defended from a deconstructionist perspective, but that defence cannot be logically derived from constitutive openness – something more has to be added to the argument. Precisely because of the undecidability inherent in constitutive openness, ethico-political moves different from or even opposite to a democracy 'to come' can be made – for instance, since there is ultimate undecidability and, as a result, no immanent tendency of the structure to closure and full presence, to sustain that closure has to be *artificially* brought about from the outside. In that way a case for totalitarianism can be presented starting from deconstructionist premises. Of course, the totalitarian argument would be as much a *non sequitur* as the argument for democracy: either direction is equally possible given the situation of structural undecidability.

We have so far presented our argument concerning the non-connection between structural undecidability and ethical injunction, starting from the 'ontological' side. But if we move to the 'normative' side, the conclusions are remarkably similar. Let us suppose, for the sake of the argument, that openness to the heterogeneity of the other is an *ethical* injunction. If one takes this proposition at face value, one is forced to conclude that we have to accept the other as different *because* she is different, whatever the content of that heterogeneity would be. This does not sound much like an ethical injunction but like ethical nihilism. And if the argument is reformulated by saying that openness to the other does not necessarily mean passive acceptance of her but rather active engagement which includes criticizing her, attacking her, even killing her, the whole argument starts to seem rather vacuous: what else do people do all the time without any need for an ethical injunction?

Yet I think that deconstruction *has* important consequences for both ethics and politics. These consequences, however, depend on deconstruction's ability to go down to the bottom of its own radicalism and avoid becoming entangled in all the problems of a Levinasian ethics (whose proclaimed aim, to present ethics as *first* philosophy, should from the start look suspicious to any deconstructionist). I see the matter this way. Undecidability should be literally taken as that condition from which no course of action necessarily follows. This means that we should not make it the necessary source of *any* concrete decision in the ethical or political sphere. In a first movement deconstruction extends undecidability – that is that which makes the decision necessary – to deeper and larger areas of social relations. The role of deconstruction is, from this perspective, to *reactivate* the moment of decision that underlies any *sedimented* set of social relations. The political and ethical significance of this first movement is that, by enlarging the area of structural undecidability, it also enlarges the area of responsibility – that is of the decision. (In Derridian terms:

the requirements of justice become more complex and multifaceted *vis-à-vis* law.)

But this first movement is immediately balanced by another one of the opposite sign, which is also essential to deconstruction. To think of undecidability as a bottomless abyss that underlies any self-sufficient 'presence' would still maintain too much of the imagery of the 'ground'. The duality undecidability/decision is something that simply belongs to the logic of any structural arrangement. Degrounding is, in this sense, also part of an operation of grounding except that this grounding is no longer to refer something back to a foundation which would act as a principle of derivation but, instead, to reinscribe that something within the terrain of the undecidables (iteration, re-mark, difference, etcetera) that make its emergence possible. So, to go back to our problem, it is no longer a question of finding a ground from which an ethical injunction should be *derived* (even less to make such a ground of undecidability itself). We live as *bricoleurs* in a plural world, having to take decisions within incomplete systems of rules (incompletion here means undecidability), and some of these rules are ethical ones. It is because of this constitutive incompletion that decisions have to be taken, but because we are faced with incompletion and not with total dispossession, the problem of a *total* ethical grounding – either through the opening to the otherness of the other, or through any similar metaphysical principle – never arises. 'The time is out of joint' but, because of that, there is never a beginning – or an end – of time. Democracy does not need to be – and cannot be – radically grounded. We can move to a more democratic society only through a plurality of acts of democratization. The consummation of time – as Derrida knows well – never arrives. Not even as a regulative idea.

This leaves us, however, with a problem: how to conceive of emancipation within this framework. What kind of collective reaggregation is open to us once we have moved away from the eschatological dimension of the classical emancipatory model? This will be my last discussion, and I will broach it by locating Derrida's intervention within the tradition of critique and reformulation of Marxism:

The Question of the Tradition

Derrida very cogently maintains that one thinks only from within a tradition, and shows that this thinking is possible only if one conceives one's relation with that past as a critical reception. Now, the reception of Marxism since the turn of the century has, in my view, turned around the discussion of two capital and interrelated issues: (1) how to make compatible – if it can be done at all – the various contradictory aspects of Marx's thought, as in Derrida's version, which relates the 'ontological' and the 'phantasmatic'; (2) how to think forms of reaggregation of political wills and social demands once the obviousness of the identification of the working class with the emancipatory agency started to dissolve. It is my contention that the deconstructionist intervention represents a crucial turn in connection with both issues. To show this, let us recapitulate the broad lines of the main classical attempts at recasting Marxism:

1. A first tendency represents the accentuation of the ontological dimension (in the Derridian sense) of Marx's thought. The absolute reconciliation of society with itself will arrive as a result of the elimination of all forms of distorted representation. The latter will be the consequence of the proletarian revolution. This tendency can be found in a vulgar materialist version (for example, Plekhanov) or in an apparently more 'superstructuralist' one, centred in the notion of 'false consciousness' (as in Lukács). Here there is no reaggregation of collective wills (the revolutionary agent is the working class), and human emancipation is fixed in its contents by a full-fledged eschatology.

2. The various forms of 'ethical' socialism to be found in Bernstein and in some currents of Austro-Marxism. The common feature of all these tendencies is a return to a Kantian dualism. Here the ontological dimension becomes weaker: the 'necessary laws of history' become more erratic, the agent of emancipation becomes more contingent and indeterminate, and the *Endziel* loses most of its eschatological precision. However, the determinacy which has been lost at the level of an objective history is retrieved at the level of an ethical regulative idea. The moment of the political decision is as absent as in Marxist orthodoxy.

3. The Sorelian-Gramscian tradition; it is here that the phantasmatic dimension finally takes the upper hand. The anchoring of social representations in the ontological bedrock of an objective history starts dissolving. The unity of the class is, for Sorel, a mythical unity. For Gramsci, the unity of a collective will results from the constitutive role of an organic ideology. History becomes an open and contingent process that does not reflect any deeper underlying reality. Two aspects are important for us: (a) the link between concrete material forces and the function that they fulfil in the classical Marxist scheme becomes loose and indeterminate. 'Collective will', 'organic ideology', hegemonic group', and so forth become empty forms that can be filled by any imaginable political and social content. They are certainly anchored in a dialectics of emancipation but, as the latter is not necessarily linked to any particular content, it becomes something like an 'existential' of historical life and is no longer the announcement of a concrete event. Now, is this not something like a deconstruction of eschatological messianism: the automization of the messianic promise from the contents that it is attached to in 'actually existing' messianisms? (b) the distinction between the ethical and the political is blurred. The moment of the ethico-political is presented as a unity. This can, of course, be given a Hegelian interpretation, but my argument is that what is really at stake in Gramsci's intervention is a politicization of ethics, in so far as the acts of institution of the social link are contingent acts of decision that presuppose relations of power. This is what gives an 'ontological' primacy to politics and to 'hegemony' as the logic governing any political intervention.

I have said enough to make it clear that, for me, it is only as an extension and radicalization of this last tendency that deconstruction can present itself both as a moment of its inscription in the Marxist tradition as well as a point of turning/deepening/supersession of the latter. My optimistic reading of *Spectres of Marx* is that it represents a step forward in the prosecution of this task. The main stumbling block that I still see to this being accomplished – at least as far as Derrida is concerned – is that the ambiguity previously pointed out between undecidability as a terrain of radicalization of the decision, and undecidability as the source of an ethical injunction is still hovering in Derrida's texts. Once this ambiguity is superseded, however, deconstruction can become one of the most powerful tools at hand for thinking strategically.

This rethinking of politics in a deconstructive fashion can (if we start from the Marxist tradition) produce three types of effect. In the first place, if we are thinking in terms of the third tendency within Marxism, we can recast and extend its system of categories far beyond the intellectual tools to which Sorel and Gramsci had access. This recasting in terms of the logic of *différance* can open the way to much more refined forms of strategic thinking.

Second, the logics of hegemonic reaggregation face, in the contemporary world, much more serious challenges than those that a Gramsci was confronted with. Our societies are far less homogeneous than those in which the Marxian models were formulated, and the constitution of the collective wills takes place in terrains crossed by far more complex relations of power – as a result, *inter alia*, of the development of mass media. The dissolution of the metaphysics of presence is not a purely intellectual operation. It is profoundly inscribed in the whole experience of recent decades. Deconstruction, as a result, faces the challenge of reinscribing the Marxian model in this complex experience of present-day society.

Finally, operating deconstructively within Marx's texts can help in a third vitally important task: reinscribing Marxism itself and each of its discursive components as a partial moment in the wider history of emancipatory discourses. Derrida is quite right to combat the current amnesia of the Marxist tradition. But let us not make the opposite mistake and think that the history of Marxism overlaps with the history of emancipatory projects. Many more ghosts than those of Marx are actually visiting and revisiting us. Benjamin's angel should become a symbol constantly reminding us of our complex and multilayered tradition. I remember that during my childhood in Argentina, in the continuous performance cinemas there was an announcement saying, 'The performance begins when you arrive'. Well, I think that 'emancipation' is the opposite: it is a performance at which we always arrive late and which forces us to guess, painfully, about its mythical or impossible origins. We have, however, to engage ourselves in this impossible task, which is, among other things, what gives deconstruction its meaning.

Note

1. The basic formulation concerning the concept of hegemony can be found in Laclau and Mouffe, *Hegemony and Socialist Strategy*, chapters 3 and 4. I have reformulated the basic dimensions of this concept, linking it more closely to the category of 'dislocation', in *New Reflections on the Revolution of Our Time*.

Bibliography

Critchley, Simon. 'On Derrida's Spectres of Marx', Society for Phenomenology and Existential Philosophy, Seattle, October 1994. Forthcoming in *Philosophy and Social Criticism*.

Derrida, Jacques. 'Force of Law: The "Mystical Foundation of Authority."' in Drucilla Cornell et al.(eds.), *Deconstruction and the Possibility of Justice*, New York, Routledge 1992.

Spectres of Marx: The State of the Debt, the Work of Mourning, and the New International, trans. Peggy Kamuf, New York, Routledge 1994.

Laclau, Ernesto. *New Reflections on the Revolution of Our Time*, London, Verso 1990.

Laclau, Ernesto, and Chantal Mouffe. *Hegemony and Socialist Strategy*, London, Verso 1985.

6

Power and Representation

The aim of this essay is to explore some of the consequences that follow – for both political theory and political action – from what has been called our 'postmodern condition'. There is today the widespread feeling that the exhaustion of the great narratives of modernity, the blurring of the boundaries of the public spaces, the operation of logics of undecidability, which seem to be robbing all meaning from collective action, are leading to a generalized retreat from the political. I would like to try to explore this claim and shall do so by considering, as my starting point, some of the most fundamental assumptions of the modern approach to politics. From the point of view of the *meaning* of any significant political intervention, there was in modernity the generalized conviction that the former had to take place at the level of the *ground* of the social – that is that politics had the means to carry out a *radical transformation* of the social, whether such a transformation was conceived as a founding revolutionary act, as an orderly set of bureaucratic measures proceeding from an enlightened elite, or as a single act opening the way to the operation of those mechanisms whose automatic unfolding would be sufficient to produce a 'society effect'. There is, in addition, the question of the *framework* that allows a conceptual grasp on such a political intervention. This was provided by the notion of *social totality* and by the series of causal connections that necessarily followed from it. As has been pointed out,[1] if we take Machiavelli and Hobbes as opposite poles in the modern approach to politics – the first centring his analysis in a theory of strategic calculation *within* the social, the second in the mechanisms-producing society as a totality – it is the Hobbesian approach that has constituted the mainstream of modern political theory. This leads us to a third feature of political action as conceived in the modern age: its radical *representability*. It could not have been otherwise; if there is a ground of the social – which is a condition of its intelligibility – and if, as a result, society can only be considered as an orderly series of effects, that is as a totality, then an action whose meaning derives from such a ground and such a totality has to be fully transparent to itself and thus endowed with limitless representability. As well, this transparency and representability had to be necessarily translated to the *agent* of the historical transformation. A limited historical actor could only carry out a universal task in so far as he was denied access to the meaning of his actions, in so far as his consciousness was a 'false' one. But as both Hegel and Marx knew well, a social totality that lacks the mirror of its own representation is an incomplete social totality and, consequently, not a social totality at all. Only full reconciliation between substance and subject, between being and knowledge, can cancel the distance between the rational and the real. But, in that case, representation is a necessary moment in the self-constitution of the totality, and the latter is only achieved so long as the distinction between action and representation is abolished. Only a limitless historical actor – a 'universal class' – can make this abolition actual. This dual movement, by which the ground becomes subject through a universal class that abolishes all 'alienation' in the forms of representation and by which the subject becomes ground by abolishing all external limitations posed by the object, is at the centre of the modern view of history and society.

These four features converge in a fifth one that could perhaps be considered the true horizon of the modern approach to politics: once the last foundation of politics is made fully visible, power becomes a purely appariential phenomenon. The reasons for this reduction are clear: if one social group exercises power over another, this power will be experienced by the second group as irrational; but if history is, however, a purely rational process, the irrationality of power must be purely appariential. In that case, either historical rationality belongs to the discourse of the dominant groups – and the claims of the oppressed are the necessary but distorted expression of a higher rationality that generates, as its own condition of possibility, an area of opaqueness; or the discourses of the oppressed are the ones that contain the seeds of a higher rationality – in which case, their full realization involves the elimination of any opaqueness (and therefore any power). In the first case, coercion and opaqueness are indeed present; but, as the power of the dominant group is fully rational, the resistance to power cannot be external but must be internal to power itself; in that case, the coercion and opaqueness of the brute fact of domination can only be the necessary appariential forms through which the rationality of power takes shape. If a system of domination is rational, its repressive character can only be appariential. This leaves us with only two alternatives: either the gaze of the dominant group is fully rational, in which case that group is a limitless historical actor, or the gazes of both the dominant and the dominated groups are partial and limited ones, in which case, the attributes of full rationality are automatically transferred to the historical analyst. The important point is that in both cases, reality of power and representability of history are in inverse relationship.

These distinctive features of modernity are so deeply entrenched in our usual forms of conceiving society and history that recent attempts to call them into question (what has been called, in very general terms, 'postmodernity') have given rise to a tendency to substitute them for their pure absence by a simple negation of their content, a negation which continues inhabiting the intellectual terrain that those positive features had delineated. Thus, the negation that there is a ground out of which all social contents obtain a precise meaning can be easily transformed into the assertion that society is entirely meaningless; questioning the universality of the agents of historical transformation leads quite often to the proposition that all historical intervention is equally and hopelessly limited; and showing the opaqueness of the process of representation is usually considered equivalent to a denial that representation is possible at all. It is, of course, easy to show that – in a fundamental sense – these nihilistic positions continue inhabiting the intellectual terrain from which they try to distance themselves. To assert, for instance, that something is meaningless is to assert a very classical conception of meaning, adding only that it is absent. But in a more important sense, it is possible to show that these apparently radical reversals can only acquire whatever force of conviction they carry by a clearly detectable inconsistency. If I conclude – as I will later in this text – that no pure relation of representation is obtainable because it is of the essence of the process of representation that the representative has to contribute to the identity of what is represented, then this cannot be transformed without inconsistency into the proposition that 'representation' is a concept that should be abandoned. For in that case, we would be left with the nude identities of the represented and the representative as self-sufficient ones, which is precisely the assumption that the whole critique of the notion of representation was questioning. In the same way, the critique of the notion of 'universality' implicit in the idea of a universal agent cannot be transformed into the assertion of the equally uniform limitation of all agents – because we could then ask ourselves, limitation in relation to what? And the answer can only be that it is in terms of a structure that equally limits *all* agents and that, in this sense, it assumes the role of a true universality. Finally, in order to be radically meaningless, something requires, as its condition of possibility, the contrastive presence of a full-fledged meaning. Meaninglessness grows out of meaning or, as has been asserted in a proposition that stated exactly the same, meaning grows out of non-meaning.

Against these movements of thought, which remain within the terrain of modernity by simply inverting its fundamental tenets, I would like to suggest an alternative strategy: instead of inverting the contents of modernity, to *deconstruct* the terrain that makes the alternative modernity/postmodernity possible. That is, instead of remaining within a polarization whose options are entirely governed by the basic categories of modernity, to show that the latter do not constitute an essentially unified block but are rather the sedimented result of a series of contingent articulations. To reactivate the intuition of the contingent character of these articulations will thus produce a widening of horizons, in so far as other articulations – equally contingent – will also show their possibility. This involves, on the one hand, a new attitude towards modernity: not a radical break with it but a new modulation of its themes; not an abandonment of its basic tenets but a hegemonization of them from a different perspective. This also involves, on the other hand, an expansion of the field of politics instead of its retreat

– a widening of the field of structural undecidability that opens the way to an enlargement of the field of political decision. It is here that 'deconstruction' and 'hegemony' show their complementarity as the two sides of a single operation. It is these two sides that I shall discuss now.

Let me start by referring to one of the originary texts of deconstruction: the analysis of the relation between meaning and knowledge in Husserl (the 'formalist' and the 'intuitionist' sides of his approach), as presented by Derrida in *Speech and Phenomena*. Husserl, in a first movement, emancipates meaning from the necessity of fulfilling it with the intuition of an object. That is, he emancipates meaning from knowledge. An expression such as 'square circle' has indeed a meaning: it is such a meaning that allows me to say that it refers to an impossible object. Meaning and object fulfilment, as a result, do not necessarily require each other. Moreover, Derrida concludes that if meaning can be strictly differentiated from knowledge, the essence of meaning is better shown when such fulfilment does not take place. But, in a second movement, Husserl quickly closed the possibilities that this breach established between knowledge and meaning had just opened:

> In other words, the genuine and true meaning is the will to say the truth. This subtle shift incorporates the *eidos* into the *telos*, and the language into knowledge. A speech could well be in conformity with its essence as speech when it is false; it nonetheless attains its entelechy when it is true. One can *speak* in saying 'The circle is square'; one speaks *well*, however, in saying that it is not. There is already sense in the first proposition, but it would be wrong to conclude from this that sense *does not wait upon* truth. It does not await truth as expecting it; it only precedes truth as its anticipation. *In truth*, the telos which announces the fulfilment, promised for 'later', has already and beforehand opened up sense as a relation with the object.[2]

The important point – the deconstructive moment of Derrida's analysis – is that if 'meaning' and 'object intuition' are not related to each other in a teleological way, in that case – from the point of view of meaning – it is undecidable whether the latter will or will not be subordinated to knowledge. In this respect the path followed by Joyce, as Derrida points out, is very different from Husserl's. But if Husserl subordinates meaning to knowledge, and if this subordination is not required by the essence of meaning, it can only be the result of an intervention that is contingent *vis-à-vis* meaning. It is the result of what Derrida calls an 'ethico-theoretical decision' on the part of Husserl. We can see how the enlargement of the field of structural undecidability brought about by the deconstructive intervention has, at the same time, widened the terrain to be filled by the decision. Now, a contingent intervention taking place in an undecidable terrain is exactly what we have called a *hegemonic* intervention.[3]

I would like to explore in some more detail this relation of mutual implication between deconstruction and hegemony. What the deconstructive move has shown is not the actual *separation* between meaning and knowledge, because the two are closely linked in Husserl's text – in fact, the unity of the latter results from this double requirement by which meaning has to be both *subordinated* to and *differentiated* from knowledge. So, the deconstructive intervention shows, first, the *contingency* of a connection, and second, the contingency of a *connection*. This has an important consequence for our argument. If only the dimension of contingency was underlined, we would have merely asserted the synthetic character of the connection between two identities, each of them fully constituted in itself and not requiring anything outside itself for that full constitution. We would be in the terrain of pure dispersion, which would be a new and contradictory form of essentialism given that each one of the monadic identities should be defined in and for itself (first extreme) and that, because dispersion is, however, a form of *relation* between objects, it requires a terrain that operates as ground or condition of possibility of that dispersion (second extreme) – in which case the identities could not, after all, be monadic. So, that connection to something else is absolutely necessary for the constitution of any identity, and this connection must be of a contingent nature. In that case, it belongs to the essence of something to have contingent connections and contingency, therefore, becomes a necessary part of the essence of that something. This leads us to the following conclusions. That if having accidents is an essential feature of a substance – or, if the contingent is an essential part of the necessary – this means that there is a necessary undecidability inscribed within any structure (by 'structure' I mean a complex identity constituted by a plurality of moments). For the structure requires the contingent connections as a necessary part of its identity, but these connections – precisely because they are contingent – cannot be logically derived from any point within the structure. So, the fact that only one of the possible paths is followed, that only one of the possible contingent connections is actualized, is undecidable from within the structure. The 'structurality' of the structure, so far as it is the actualization of a series of contingent connections, cannot find the source of these connections within itself. This is why in Derrida's analysis, Husserl's ethico-theoretical *decision* must be brought into the picture as an essential element in order to establish the subordination of meaning to knowledge. An *external* source of a certain set of structural connections is what we will call *force*.[4]

This is exactly the point at which deconstruction and hegemony cross each other. For if deconstruction discovers the role of the decision out of the undecidability of the structure, hegemony as a theory of the decision taken in an undecidable terrain requires that the contingent character of the connections existing in that terrain is fully shown by deconstruction. The category of hegemony emerged in order to think about the political character of social relations in a theoretical arena that had seen the collapse of the classical Marxist conception of the 'dominant class' – the latter conceived as a necessary and immanent effect of a fully constituted structure. The hegemonic articulations were from the beginning conceived as contingent, precarious and pragmatic constructions. This is why, in Gramsci, there is a sustained effort to break with the identification of hegemonic agencies to objective social positions within the structure. His notion of 'collective will' tries precisely to effect this break, so far as the collective wills are conceived as unstable social agencies, with imprecise and constantly redefined boundaries, and constituted through the contingent articulation of a plurality of social identities and relations. The two central features of a hegemonic intervention are, in this sense, the *contingent* character of the hegemonic articulations and their *constitutive* character, in the sense that they institute social relations in a primary sense, not depending on any a priori social rationality.

This, however, poses two problems. The first refers to the external instance that takes the decision. Is this not to reintroduce a new essentialism via the subject? Is it not to replace an objective closure of the structure by a subjective closure through the intervention of the agent? The second problem concerns the conditions of visibility of the contingency of the structure. For reasons that will become apparent in a moment, these two problems must be tackled successively, as in the order just presented.

Regarding the first point, it is obvious that the matter cannot be solved on the basis of simply asserting that the trick is done by a subject who rearticulates around its project the dispersed elements of a dislocated structure. There is, in fact, a far more complex relation between subject and structure than the one that this simplistic version of what is involved in a hegemonic articulation suggests. For the obvious question arises: who is the subject and what is the terrain of its constitution? If we want to avoid facile *deus ex machina* solutions, this question must be answered. A first answer would be in terms of a well-mannered and 'enlightened' Marxism: there is a primary terrain on which social agencies are constituted – the relations of production – and a secondary terrain on which the dispersed elements to be hegemonized operate. In this way, we are in the best of both worlds: we can assert the full role of agency in doing the articulating job without falling into any *demodé* subjectivism; we can maintain the notion of a fundamental agent of historical change without renouncing the multiform and rich variety of social life; we can give free rein to the intriguing game of historical contingency knowing that we have the disciplinary means to bring them back – 'in the last instance' – to the stern world of structural constraints. What a beautiful and tidy little world! The drawback to the picture is, of course, that if the separation between the two levels has any validity at all, then we have to make explicit the totality within which that separation takes place; and if there is such a totality, contingency cannot be true contingency. For if the *limits* of the contingent are necessary, then these limits are part of the contingent identity. Conversely, as the necessary limits are limits of the contingent variation, the presence of that variation is absolutely necessary for the existence of the limits and in that case, as we asserted earlier, contingency becomes necessary. The world is, after all, more wild and unforeseeable than the tidy blueprints of our *bien pensant* Marxist.

So, let us mix the cards and start the game again. The hegemonic subject cannot have a terrain of constitution different from the structure to which it belongs. But, however, if the subject was a mere subject position within the structure, the latter would be fully closed and there would be no contingency at all – and no need to hegemonize anything. The terms of our problem are the following: hegemony means *contingent* articulation; contingency means *externality* of the articulating force *vis-à-vis* the articulated elements, and this externality cannot be thought of as an actual separation of levels within a fully constituted totality because that is no externality at all. So, how are we to account for an externality emerging within the structure in a way that is not the result of a positive differentiation of its constitutive levels? This can only happen if the structure is not fully reconciled with itself, if it is inhabited by an original lack, by a radical undecidability that needs to be constantly superseded by acts of decision. These acts are precisely what constitute the *subject*, who can only exist as a will transcending the structure. Because this will has no place of constitution external to the structure but is the result of the failure of the structure to constitute itself, it can be formed only through acts of identification. If I need to identify with something, it is because I do not have a full identity in the first place. These acts of identification can only be thought of as the result of the lack within the structure and have the permanent trace of that lack. Contingency is shown in this way: as the inherent distance of the structure from itself. (This is, in fact, the matrix of all visibility and of all representation: without this distance no vision would be possible.)

This leads us to our second problem: what are the conditions for visibility of the contingency of the structure? Part of the question has actually been answered: in so far as no specific content is *predetermined* to fill the structural gap, it is the conflict between various contents in their attempt to play this filling role that will make the contingency of the structure visible. But this leads to another consequence, which is of greater importance for our argument. The visibility of the contingent character of the content that closes the structure requires that such a content is seen as indifferent to the structural gap and, in that sense, as equivalent to other possible contents. This means that the relation between the concrete content and its role as filler of the gap within the structure is purely external – that is precisely where the contingency lies. But in that case, the concrete content that does the filling will be constitutively split: on the one hand, it will be its own literal content; on the other – so far as it fulfils a function that is contingent *vis-à-vis* that control – it will represent a general function of filling that is independent of any particular content. This second function is what, in another text, I have called *the general form of fullness*.[5] Thus, the complete answer to our second problem would be that the condition for visibility of the contingency of the structure is visibility of the gap between the general form of fullness and the concrete content that incarnates that form. In a situation of great disorder, the need for an order becomes more pressing than the concrete content of the latter; and the more generalized the disorder, the greater will be the distance between these two dimensions and the more indifferent people will be to the concrete content of the political forms that bring things back to a certain normality.[6]

We can now draw some general conclusions about this split. It is easy to see that were a total closure of the structure to be achieved, the split would be superseded because, in that case, the general form of the fullness would be immanent to the structure and it would be impossible to differentiate it from the concrete – literal – content of the latter. It is only if the fullness is perceived as that which the structure lacks that general form and concrete content can be differentiated. In that case, we would apparently be left with a simple duality by which we would have, on the one hand, the (partially destructured) structure and, on the other, the various and – as we have seen – partially equivalent attempts to fill the structural gaps, to introduce new restructuring discourses and practices. There is, however, a sleight of hand in this way of presenting the matter, by which something essentially important is concealed. Let us examine the matter carefully. Everything turns around the status of this category of 'equivalence', which we have introduced to characterize one of the dimensions of the relationship between the various discourses that try to fill the structural gap. What is the condition of possibility of such an equivalence? Let us think of the well-known example of people who live in the neighbourhood of a waterfall. They live hearing all their lives the noise of the water falling – that is, the sound is a permanent background of which they are normally unaware. So they do not *actually* hear the noise. But if for any reason the fall of the water suddenly stops one day, they will start hearing that which, strictly speaking, cannot be heard: silence. It is the lack of something that has thus acquired full presence. Now, let us suppose that this silence is intermittently interrupted by noises of different origin that the fall of the water had made inaudible before. All these sounds will have a split identity: on the one hand they are *specific* noises; on the other, they have the equivalent identity of *breaking* the silence. The noises are only equivalent because there is silence; but the silence is only audible as the lack of a former fullness.

This example, however, misses one dimension of the communitarian lack: the latter is experienced as deprivation, while I can be perfectly indifferent to the presence or absence of the noise of the fall. This is why the social lack will be lived as disorder, as disorganization, and attempts to supersede it will exist via identifications. But if social relations are discursive relations, symbolic relations that constitute themselves through processes of signification, then the failure of this process of constitution, the presence of the lack within the structure, must itself be signified. So the question is, are there specific discursive forms of presence of the lack? Does this split between concrete content and general form of fullness have specific ways of showing itself? The answer is yes, and I will argue that the general form of fullness shows itself through the discursive presence of floating signifiers that are constitutively so – that is, they are not the result of contingent ambiguities of meaning but of the need to signify the lack (the absent fullness within the structure). Let us suppose a political discourse asserting that 'Labour is more capable than the Tory Party to ensure the *unity of the British people*'. In a proposition like this, which is fairly common in political argument, we have an entity – 'unity of the British people' – that is qualitatively different from the other two – Labour and the Tories. First, this unity is something to be achieved, so that, contrary to the other two entities, it is not something actually existent but the name of an absent fullness. But second, the kind of political unity that Labour and the Tories would bring about would be substantially different, so that if the term *unity* meant a concrete entity at the same level of the two political forces, the proposition would be almost tautological – it would be equivalent to 'Labour is more capable than the Tories to ensure a Labour kind of unity of the British people'. But obviously the original proposition does not intend to say *that*. So on the one hand, the various political forces provide the concrete content of the unity, without which the unity cannot exist, but, on the other hand, that unity is not fully exhausted by any of these alternative concrete contents. 'Unity' is a floating signifier because its signifieds are fixed only by the concrete contents provided by the antagonistic forces; but, at the same time, this floating is not a purely contingent and circumstantial one, because without it political argument would be impossible and political life would be a dialogue between the deaf, in which we would only have incommensurable propositions. The basic split mentioned earlier finds the form of its discursive presence through this production of empty signifiers representing the general form of fullness. In another essay,[7] I have shown that if an expression such as 'the fascists succeeded in carrying out the revolution in which the communists failed' made any sense in Italy in the early 1920s, it is because the signifier 'revolution' was an empty one, representing people's feeling that the old order coming from the Risorgimento was obsolete and that a radical refoundation of the Italian state was needed.

Let us take one last example. In an article published some years ago,[8] Quentin Skinner takes issue with the way Stuart Hampshire presents an imaginary dialogue between a liberal and a Marxist.[9] According to Hampshire the disagreement turns around the meaning of the term *political*: the Marxist gives to it an extensive application while liberal use is far more restricted. For Skinner, however, much more than the meaning of the term is involved in the dispute, given that it is not at all clear why incommensurable meanings attributed to a term would establish a criterion for preferring one to the other. And he concludes:

> If the Marxist is genuinely to persuade the Liberal to share or at least acknowledge some political insight, he needs in effect to make two points. One is of course that the term political can appropriately be applied to a range of actions where the Liberal has never thought of applying it. But the other, which his application of the term challenges the Liberal to admit, is that this is due not to a disagreement about

the meaning of the term but rather to the fact that the Liberal is a person of blinkered political sensitivity and awareness.[10]

I agree with Skinner's two points, but I would like to add something concerning the kind of dialogical process that the two operations involve. To convince the liberal that the term *political* can be applied to a range of actions that it had not encompassed before is something that can be done, as Skinner himself points out, only if the Marxist were able to claim with some plausibility that he or she is employing the term in virtue of its *agreed* sense.[11] Now, if the liberal does not perceive that this agreed sense encompasses the kind of situation that the Marxist is referring to, this could be for one of two reasons: either because of a *logical* mistake or, more plausibly, because of a 'blinkered political sensitivity and awareness'. So, Skinner's two points are not really different from each other; to apply a term to a new range of actions on the basis of an agreed sense requires, as a *sine qua non* condition, a *redescription* of a given situation in terms that do away with blinkered political sensitivity. But with this we have advanced very little. For why would a redescription be accepted at all? If somebody is perfectly happy and well-installed in a description A, he or she has no reason whatsoever to move to another description B. The only way out of this impasse is if the description B does not come to replace a full-fledged description A, but provides a description to a situation that had become increasingly undescribable in terms of the old paradigm. That is, the only way the process of conviction can operate is if it moves from lack of conviction to conviction, not from one conviction to another. This means that the function of a new language is to fill a gap. So, Hampshire is correct in thinking that there is no possibility of choice between two separate worlds of thought; but Skinner is also correct in maintaining that the dispute is not just about the meaning of the terms but about wider redescriptions. If we agreed that the condition of a successful redescription is that it not only replaces an old one but also fills a gap opened in the general describability of a situation, then the valid redescription will have a split identity: on the one hand, it will be its own content; on the other, it will embody the principle of describability as such – that is what we have called the general form of fullness. Without this second order of signification, without what we could call the hegemonization of the general form of describability by a concrete description, we would be in Hampshire's 'separate worlds of thought', and no interaction between political discourses would be possible.

The previous developments provide some elements to address our initial question: how can the historical horizon of modernity be transcended without falling into the trap of an exclusive alternative modernity/postmodernity in which the purely negative character of the contents of the second pole means that those of the first continue dominating unchallenged? How to go beyond a nihilism whose very logic reproduces precisely that which it wants to question? Our argument will be, first, that it is the structural undecidability discussed in the preceeding pages, when accepted in all its radical consequences, that makes it possible to go beyond both modernity and its nihilistic reverse; and second, that this going beyond modernity consists not in an abandonment of all its contents but rather in the loss of its dimension of horizon (a category that I must explain). I shall discuss the first point in connection with the operation of the logics of representation and power in contemporary societies and shall move later to the question of the crisis of the basic horizon of modernity.

Representation first: what is involved in a process of representation? Essentially the *fictio iuris* that somebody is present in a place from which he or she is materially absent. The representation is the process by which somebody else – the representative – 'substitutes for' and at the same time 'embodies' the represented. The conditions for a perfect representation, would be met, it seems, when the representation is a direct process of transmission of the will of the represented, when the act of representation is totally transparent in relation to that will. This presupposes that the will is fully constituted and that the role of the representative is exhausted in its function of intermediation. Thus the opaqueness inherent in any substitution and embodiment must be reduced to a minimum; the body in which the incarnation takes place must be almost invisible. This is, however, the point at which the difficulties start. For from neither the side of the representative nor that of the represented do the conditions of a perfect representation obtain – and this is a result not of what is empirically attainable but of the very logic inherent in the process of representation. So far as the represented is concerned, if he or she needs to be represented at all, this is the result of the fact that his or her basic identity is constituted in a place *A* and that decisions that can affect this identity will be taken in a place *B.* But in that case his or her identity is an incomplete identity, and the relation of representation – far from referring to full-fledged identity – is a *supplement* necessary for the constitution of that identity. The crucial problem is to determine whether this supplement can simply be *deduced* from the place *A,* where the original identity of the represented was constituted, or if it is an entirely *new* addition, in which case, the identity of the represented is transformed and enlarged through the process of representation. It is my view that the latter is always the case. Let us take a very simple example, in which the contribution of the representative to the constitution of the 'interest' to be represented is apparently minimal: a deputy representing a group of farmers whose overriding interest is maintaining the prices of agricultural products. Even in this case, the role of the representative far exceeds the simple transmission of a preconstituted interest. For the terrain on which this interest must be represented is that of national politics, where many other things are taking place, and even something apparently as simple as the protection of agricultural prices requires processes of negotiation and articulation with a whole series of forces and problems that far exceeds what is thinkable and deducible from place *A.* So, the representative *inscribes* an interest in a complex reality different from that in which the interest was originally formulated and, in doing so, he or she constructs and transforms that interest. But the representative is thus also transforming the identity of the represented. The original gap in the identity of the represented, which needed to be filled by a supplement contributed by the process of representation, opens an undecidable movement in two directions that is constitutive and irreducible. There is an opaqueness, an essential impurity in the process of representation, which is at the same time its condition of both possibility and impossibility. The 'body' of the representative cannot be reduced for essential reasons. A situation of perfect accountability and transmission in a transparent medium would not involve any representation at all.

So, the idea of having a perfect representation involves a

logical impossibility – but this does not mean that representation is *entirely* impossible. The problem, rather, is that representation is the name of an undecidable game that organizes a variety of social relations but whose operations cannot be fixed in a rationally graspable and ultimately univocal mechanism. Representation has been criticized very often in democratic theory for the difficulties it poses for an accountability that is considered essential in a democratic society. But most versions of this criticism are ill-grounded. To see the danger only in the possibility that the will of a constituency is ignored or betrayed by its representative is a one-sided view. There are, of course, many cases in which such will is ignored and many cases of systematic distortion. But what this criticism ignores is the role of the representative in the constitution of such a will. If, as I stated, there is a gap in the identity of the represented that requires the process of representation to fill it, it is simply not true that the reduction of the social areas in which representative mechanisms operate will necessarily lead to more democratically managed societies. We live in societies in which we are increasingly less able to refer to a single or primary level as the one on which the basic identity of social agents is constituted. This means, on the one hand, that social agents are becoming more and more 'multiple selves', with loosely integrated and unstable identities; and on the other, that there is a proliferation of the points in society from which decisions affecting their lives will be taken. As a result, the need to 'fill in the gaps' is no longer a 'supplement' to be added to a basic area of constitution of the identity of the agent but, instead, becomes a *primary* terrain. The constitutive role of representation in the formation of the will, which was partly concealed in more stable societies, now becomes fully visible. The level of national polities, for instance, can operate as one on which the discourses of the representatives propose forms of articulation and unity between otherwise fragmented identities. This means that we cannot escape the framework of the representative processes, and that democratic alternatives must be constructed that multiply the points from and around which representation operates rather than attempt to limit its scope and area of operation.

We have seen what is involved in a situation in which the discourse of the representative must fill the gap in the identity of the represented: that discourse will have the dual role, to which I referred before, of both being a particular filler and symbolizing the filling function. But this means that the gap between the two terms of this duality will necessarily increase in present-day societies and that the role of the 'representatives' will be ever more central and constitutive. Is that really so bad? Are we increasingly distancing ourselves, through that developing gap, from the possibility of having democratically managed societies? I do not think so. The situation is rather the reverse. In a situation in which concrete content and general form of fullness cannot be differentiated – that is in a closed universe in which no representation is required – no democratic competition is possible. The transparency of a fully-acquired identity will be the automatic source of all decisions. This is the world of the Homeric heroes. But if there is a gap in the identity of social actors, the filling of this gap will necessarily generate the split between filling content and filling function and, because the latter is not necessarily associated with any content, there will be a competition between the various contents to incarnate the very form of fullness. A democratic society is not one in which the 'best' content dominates un-challenged but, rather, one in which nothing is definitely acquired and there is always the possibility of challenge. If we think, for instance, of the resurgence of nationalism and all kinds of ethnic identities in present-day Eastern Europe, then we can easily see that the danger for democracy lies in the closure of these groups around fully-fledged identities that can only reinforce their most reactionary tendencies and create the conditions for a permanent confrontation with other groups. It is, on the contrary, the integration of these nations into wider ensembles – such as the EU – that can create the bases for a democratic development, and that requires the split from oneself, the need to be represented outside oneself to be a proper self. There is democracy only if there is the recognition of the positive value of a dislocated identity. The term *hybridization* aptly proposed by Homi Bhabha and other writers is fully applicable here. But in that case, the condition of a democratic society is constitutive incompletion – which involves, of course, the impossiblity of an ultimate grounding. We can see that this is a degrounding that escapes the perverse and sterile modernity/nihilism dichotomy: it confronts us not with the alternative presence/absence of a ground but with the unending search for something that has to give a positive value to its very impossibility.

We are in the same situation if we refer to power. The traditional notion of an emancipated society is that of a fully rational society from which power has been entirely eliminated. But as we have seen, power must, for the rationalistic conception of society on which the notion of emancipation is based, be purely appariential. This presents us with the terms of an antinomian situation. If emancipation is to be possible as a *real* event – that is if it is to have an ontological status and not be just the lived content of the false consciousness of people – then power must also be real. But if power is real, the relation between power and that which emancipates itself from it must be one of radical exteriority – otherwise there would be a rational link leading from power to emancipation, and emancipation would not be truly so. The difficulty lies in the fact that a relation of radical exteriority between two forces is a *contingent* relation and, consequently, if emancipation eliminates power through a contingent process of struggle, it must itself be power. Could it not be said, however, that once emancipation has destroyed power it ceases to be power? No, because full transparency and rationality cannot logically proceed from the opaqueness inherent in a contingent act of power. It is only if the overthrowing of power had been the expression of a higher rationality that had transformed it into a *necessary* step that emancipation would be rational through and through. But in that case, as we have seen, it would have ceased to be emancipation. So the very condition of emancipation – its radical break from power – is what makes emancipation impossible because it becomes indistinguishable from power. The consequence is not, however, the nihilistic result that emancipation is impossible and that only power remains, because what our conclusion asserts is that power is the very condition of emancipation. If all emancipation must constitute itself as power, there will be a plurality of powers – and, as a result, a plurality of contingent and partial emancipations. We are in the Machiavellian situation of a plurality of struggles *within* the social, not in an act of radical refoundation that would become the source of the social. What is displaced is the logically impossible idea of a radical dichotomy that makes emancipation synonymous with the elimination of power. But, as in the case of the impurity inherent in the process of representation, the dimension of power that is ineradicable and constitutive of all social identity should be seen not as a burden but as the source of a new historical optimism. For if a total elimination of power were attainable, social relations would be entirely transparent, difference would become impossible, and *freedom* would be a redundant term. We would reach, effectively, the end of history.

This leads me to my last point. What we are witnessing in our contemporary experience is the end of modernity as a horizon, but not necessarily of the particular objectives and demands that have constituted its contents. We call *horizon* that which establishes, at one and the same time, the limits and the terrain of constitution of any possible object – and that, as a result, makes impossible any 'beyond'. Reason for the Enlightenment, progress for positivism, communist society for Marxism – these are the names not of objects within a certain horizon but of the horizon itself. In this sense, the basic features of the modern conception of politics that I pointed out at the beginning of my text are firmly rooted in the main dimensions of modernity conceived as a fundamental horizon. Now, generalizing the main conclusions of my argument, I could assert that the crisis of that horizon, which has been pointed out from many quarters, has – far from leading to a generalized implosion of the social and a retreat from participation in public spheres – instead, for the first time, created the possibility of a radically political conception of society. Let us go briefly to our five features and see in what way the 'postmodern' turn helps to liberate politics from its limiting modern ties.

Radical transformation in the first place: if this transformation is conceived as taking place at the level of a rationally graspable ground of the social, then the transformation is the work of reason and not of ourselves. A rationality transcending us fully determines what is to happen, and our only possible freedom is to be conscious of necessity. It is in this respect that a universal class can be only a limitless historical actor who abolishes the subject/object duality. But if there is no ground of the social, any historical intervention will be the work of limited historical agents. This limitation, however, is more than compensated for by a new freedom that social agents win as they become the creators of their own world. As a result, the notion of radical transformation is displaced: its radical character is given by the overdetermination of partial changes that it involves, not by its operation at the level of fundamental ground. This explains why the second and fourth features that we found in the modern approach to politics are also displaced. The category of 'social totality' certainly cannot be abandoned because in so far as all social action takes place in an overdetermined terrain, it 'totalizes' social relations to some extent; but totality now becomes the name of a horizon and no longer of a ground. And, for the same reason, social actors try to overcome their limitations but, to the extent that the notion of a limitless historical actor has been abandoned, this overcoming can be only the pragmatic process of the construction of highly over-determined social identities. What about representability? It is clear that if there is no ultimate rational ground of the social, total representability is impossible. But in that case, we could speak of 'partial' representations, which, within their limits, would be more or less adequate pictures of the world. If radical contingency has occupied the terrain of the ground, any social meaning will be a social construction and not an intellectual reflection of what things 'in themselves' are. The consequence is that in this 'war of interpretations', power, far from being merely appariential, becomes constitutive of social objectivity.

Three conclusions follow from the preceding developments. The first is that politics, far from being confined to a super-structure, occupies the role of what we can call an *ontology of the social*. If politics is the ensemble of the decisions taken in an undecidable terrain – that is a terrain in which power is constitutive – then the social can consist only in the sedimented forms of a power that has blurred the traces of its own contingency. The second conclusion is that if the movement from modernity to postmodernity takes place at the level of their intellectual and social horizons, this movement will not necessarily involve the collapse of all the objects and values contained within the horizon of modernity but, instead, will involve their reformulation from a different perspective. The universal values of the Enlightenment, for instance, do not need to be abandoned but need, instead, to be presented as pragmatic social constructions and not as expressions of a necessary requirement of reason. Finally, the previous reflections show, I think, the direction into which the construction of a postmodern social imaginary should move: to indicate the positive communitarian values that follow from the limitation of historical agents, from the contingency of social relations, and from those political arrangements through which society organizes the management of its own impossibility.

Notes

1. S. R. Clegg, *Frameworks of Power*, London, Sage 1989, ch. 2.
2. Jacques Derrida, *Speech and Phenomena*, Evanston, Northwestern University Press, p. 98.
3. Ernesto Laclau and Chantal Mouffe, *Hegemony and Socialist Strategy*, London, Verso 1985.
4. This is, to some extent, the direction in which Derrida is moving in his essay 'Force and Signification', in *Writing and Difference*, Chicago, University of Chicago Press 1978.
5. In the first essay of *New Reflections on the Revolution of Our Time*, London, Verso 1990.
6. On the basis of this argument I have tried to establish a contraposition between Plato and Hobbes in ibid., pp. 68–72.
7. See chapter 7.
8. Quentin Skinner, 'Language and Social Change', in J. Tully (ed.), *Meaning and Context: Quentin Skinner and His Critics*, London, Polity Press 1988, pp. 125–6.
9. Stuart Hampshire, *Thought and Action*, London, Chatto and Windus 1959, p. 97.
10. Skinner, 'Language and Social Change', p. 126.
11. Ibid.

Community and its Paradoxes:
Richard Rorty's 'Liberal Utopia'

Anti-foundationalism has so far produced a variety of intellectual and cultural effects, but few of them have referred to the terrain of politics. It is one of the merits of Richard Rorty's work to have attempted, vigorously and persuasively, to establish such a connection. In his book, *Contingency, Irony and Solidarity* (Cambridge University Press 1989), he has presented an excellent picture of the intellectual transformation of the West during the last two centuries and, on the basis of it, has drawn the main lines of a social and political arrangement that he has called a 'liberal utopia'. It is not that Rorty tries to present his (post-) philosophical approach as a theoretical grounding for his political proposal – an attempt (which Rorty rejects) that would simply 'reoccupy' with an anti-foundationalist discourse the terrain of the lost foundation. It is rather that anti-foundationalism, together with a plurality of other narratives and cultural interventions, has created the intellectual climate in which certain social and political arrangements are thinkable.

In this essay I will try to show that, though I certainly agree with most of Rorty's philosophical arguments and positions, his notion of 'liberal utopia' presents a series of shortcomings which can only be superseded if the liberal features of Rorty's utopia are reinscribed in the wider framework of what we have called 'radical democracy'.[1]

I

Let us summarize, in the first place, the main points of Rorty's argument. At the beginning of the book he asserts his primary thesis in the following terms:

> . . . this book tries to show how things look if we drop the demand for a theory which unifies the public and private, and are content to treat the demands of self-creation and of human solidarity as equally valid, yet for ever incommensurable. It sketches a figure whom I call the 'liberal ironist'. I borrow my definition of 'liberal' from Judith Shklar, who says that liberals are the people who think that cruelty is the worst thing we do. I use 'ironist' to name the sort of person who faces up to the contingency of his or her own most central beliefs and desires – someone sufficiently historicist and nominalist to have abandoned the idea that those central beliefs and desires refer back to something beyond the reach of time and chance. Liberal ironists are people who include among these ungroundable desires their own hope that suffering will be diminished, that the humiliation of human beings by other human beings may cease.[2]

The milieu in which these objectives are attainable is that of a postmetaphysical culture.

The specifically political argument about the contingency of the community is preceded by two chapters on 'the contingency of language' and 'the contingency of selfhood' which constitute its background. Rorty points out that two hundred years ago two main changes took place in the intellectual life of Europe: the increasing realization that truth is fabricated rather than found – which made possible the utopian politics of reshaping social relations – and the Romantic revolution which led to a vision of art as self-creation rather than as imitation of reality. These changes joined forces and progressively acquired cultural hegemony. German idealism was a first attempt at drawing the intellectual consequences of this transformation, but ultimately failed as a result of confusing the idea that nothing has an internal nature to be represented with the very different one that the spatio-temporal world is a product of the human mind. What actually lies behind these dim intuitions of the Romantic period is the increasing realization that there is no intrinsic nature of the real, but that the real will look different depending on the languages with which it is described, and that there is not a meta-language or neutral language which will allow us to decide between competing first-order languages. Philosophical argument does not proceed through an internal deconstruction of a thesis presented in a certain vocabulary but rather through the presentation of a competing vocabulary:

> Interesting philosophy is rarely an examination of the pros and cons of a thesis. Usually it is, implicitly or explicitly, a contest between an entrenched vocabulary which has become a nuisance and a half-formed new vocabulary which vaguely promises great things.[3]

At this point, Rorty, faithful to his method, simply drops the old conception of language and embarks upon a new operation of redescription through Donald Davidson's philosophy of language, with its rejection of the idea that language constitutes a medium of either representation or expression, and its similarity with the Wittgensteinian conception of alternative vocabularies as alternative tools. Mary Hesse's 'metaphoric redescriptions' and Harold Bloom's 'strong poet' are also quoted in this connection.

After having shown the contingency of language, Rorty gives selfhood a turn. Here the main heroes are Nietzche and (especially) Freud. For Nietzche it is only the poet who fully perceives the contingency of self:

> . . . Western tradition thinks of a human life as a triumph just in so far as it breaks out of the world of time, appearance and idiosyncratic opinion into another world – the world of enduring truth. Nietzsche, by contrast, thinks the important boundary to cross is not the one separating time from atemporal truth but rather the one which divides the old from the new. He thinks a human life triumphant just in so far as it escapes inherited descriptions of the contingencies of its existence and finds new descriptions. This is the difference between the will to truth and the will to self-overcoming. It is the difference between thinking of redemption as making contact with something larger and more enduring than oneself and redemption as Nietzsche describes it: 'recreating all "it was" into a "thus I willed it"'.[4]

But it is Freud who represents the most important step forward in the process of de-divinization of the self. He showed the way in which all the features of our conscience can be traced back to the contingency of our upbringing:

> He de-universalizes the moral sense, making it as idiosyncratic as the poet's inventions. He thus let us see the moral consciousness as historically conditioned, a product as much of time and chance as of political or aesthetic consciousness.[5]

In spite of their many points in common, Freud is more useful, according to Rorty, than Nietzche, because the former shows that the conformist bourgeois is only dull on the surface, before the psychoanalytic exploration, while the latter relegates 'the vast majority of humanity to the status of dying animals'.[6]

Finally we reach the contingency of the community, which should be dealt with in more detail because it concerns the main topic of this essay. Rorty finds an initial difficulty here: he is attached to both liberal democracy and anti-foundationalism, but the vocabulary in which the former was initially presented is that of Enlightenment rationalism. The thesis that he tries to defend in the following two chapters is that, although this vocabulary was essential to liberal democracy in its initial stages, today it has become an impediment to its further progress and consolidation. This involves him in an effort to reformulate the democratic ideal in a non-rationalist and non-universalist way.

Rorty starts by clearing out of his way the possible charges of relativism and irrationalism. He quotes Schumpeter as saying, 'To realize the relative validity of one's convictions and yet stand for them unflinchingly, is what distinguishes a civilized man from a barbarian'; and he includes Isaiah Berlin's comment on this passage, 'To demand more than this is perhaps a deep and incurable metaphysical need: but to allow it to determine one's practice is a symptom of an equally deep, and more dangerous, moral and political immaturity'.[7] It is these assertions that Michael Sandel is brought into the picture to oppose: 'If one's convictions are only relatively valid, why stand for them unflinchingly?'[8] Thus, the relativism debate is opened in its classical terms. Rorty steps into this debate by trying to make a non-issue of relativism. He starts by discarding two notions of absolute validity: that which identifies as absolutely valid with what is valid to everyone and anyone – because in this case, there would be no interesting statement which would be absolutely valid; and that which identifies it with those statements which can be justified to all those who are not corrupted – because this presupposes a division of human nature (divine/animal) which is ultimately incompatible with liberalism. The only alternative is, as a consequence, to restrict the opposition between rational and irrational forms of persuasion to the confines of a language game, where it is possible to distinguish reasons of belief from causes for belief which are not rational. This, however, leaves open the question about the rationality of the shifts of vocabularies and, as there is no neutral ground upon which to decide between them, it looks as if all important shifts in paradigms, metaphorics or vocabularies would have causes but not reasons. But this would imply that all great intellectual movements such as Christianity, Galilean science or the Enlightenment should be considered to have irrational origins. This is the point at which Rorty concludes that the usefulness of a description in terms of the opposition rational/irrational vanishes. Davidson – whom Rorty quotes at this point – notes that once the notion of rationality has been restricted to internal coherence, if the use of the term is not also restricted, we will find ourselves calling 'irrational' many things we appreciate (the decision to repress a certain desire, for instance, will appear irrational from the point of view of the desire itself). If Davidson and Hesse are right, metaphors are causes and not reasons for changes in beliefs but this does not make them 'irrational'; it is the very notion of irrationality that has to be questioned. The consequence is that the question of validity is essentially open and conversational. Only a society in which a system of taboos and a rigid delimitation of the order of subjects has been imposed and accepted by everybody will escape the conversational nature of validity; but this is precisely the kind of society which is strictly incompatible with liberalism:

> It is central to the idea of a liberal society that, with respect to words as opposed to deeds, persuasion as opposed to force, anything goes. This open mindedness should not be fostered because, as Scripture teaches, Truth is great and will prevail, not because, as Milton suggests, Truth will always win in a free and open encounter. It should be fostered for its own sake. *A Liberal society is one which is content to call 'true' whatever the upshot of such encounters turns out to be.* That is why a liberal society is badly served by an attempt to supply it with 'philosophical foundations'. For the attempt to supply such foundations presupposes a natural order of topics and arguments which is prior to, and overrides the results of, encounters between old and new vocabularies.[9]

This question of the relationship between foundationalism (rationalism) and liberalism is treated by Rorty through a convincing critique of Horkheimer and Adorno's *Dialectic of Enlightenment*. He accepts their vision that the forces put into movement by the Enlightenment have undermined the Enlightenment's own convictions, but he does not accept their conclusions that, as a result of this, liberalism is at present intellectually and morally bankrupt. According to Rorty the vocabularies which presided over the initiation of a historical process or intellectual movement are never adopted by them when they reach maturity, and in his view ironic thinking is far more appropriate to a fully-fledged liberal society than rationalism.

The poet and the utopian revolutionary, who are central historical actors in Rorty's account, play the role of 'protesting in the name of society itself against those aspects of the society which are unfaithful to its own self-image'. And he adds in a crucial passage:

> This substitution (of the protest of alienated people by the revolutionary and the poet) seems to cancel out the difference between the revolutionary and the reformer. But one can define the *ideally* liberal society as one in which the difference *is* cancelled out. A liberal society is one whose ideals can be fulfilled by persuasion rather than force, by reform rather than revolution, by the free and open encounters of present linguistic and other practices with suggestions for new practices. But this is to say that an ideal liberal society is one which has no purpose except freedom, no goal except a willingness to see how such encounters go and to abide by the outcome. It has no purpose except to make life easier for poets and revolutionaries while seeing to it that they make life harder for others only by words, and not deeds. It is a society whose hero is the strong poet and the revolutionary because it recognizes that it is what it is, has the morality it has, speaks the language it does, not because it approximates the will of God or the nature of man but because certain poets and revolutionaries of the past spoke as they did.[10]

Rorty brings the figure of the liberal ironist into focus by comparing it with Foucault (an ironist who is not liberal) and with Habermas (a liberal who is not ironist). In the case of Foucault, there is an exclusive emphasis on self-realization, self-enjoyment. Foucault is unwilling to consider the advantages and improvements of liberal societies because he is much more concerned with the ways in which these societies still present this process of self-creation. They have even, in many senses, imposed increased controls over their members which were unknown in pre-modern societies. Rorty's main disagreement with Foucault is that, in his view, it is not necessary to create a new 'we'; 'we liberals' is enough. With Habermas the situation is the opposite. For him, it is essential that a democratic society's self-image has an element of universalism which is to be obtained through what he calls a process of domination-free communication. He tries to maintain – even if through a radical recasting – a bridge with the rationalistic foundation of the Enlightenment. So, Rorty's disagreement with Foucault is essentially political while with Habermas it is purely philosophical.

Finally, we should consider for our purposes two possible objections to Rorty's liberal utopia which he tries to answer. The first is that the abandonment of the metaphysical grounding of liberal societies will deprive them of a social glue which is indispensable for the continuation of free institutions. The second is that it is not possible – from a psychological point of view – to be a liberal ironist and, at the same time, not to have some metaphysical beliefs about the nature of human beings. Rorty's answer to the first objection is that society is not pulled together by any philosophical grounding but by common vocabularies and common hopes. The same objection was made in the past about the disastrous social effects which would derive from the masses' loss of religious beliefs, and the prophesy proved to be wrong. Ironists have been essentially elitist and have not contributed excessively to the improvement of the community. The redescription in which they engage frequently leads to attack on the most cherished values of people and to their humiliation. On top of that, though the metaphysicians also engage in redescriptions, they have the advantage over ironists in that they give to people what claims to be true in nature, a new faith to which they can adhere. But here Rorty says that the primary difficulty is that people are demanding from ironist philosophers something that philosophy cannot give: answers to questions such as 'Why not be cruel?' or 'Why be kind?' The expectation that a *theoretical* answer can be given is simply the result of a metaphysical lag. In the post-philosophical era it is the narratives which perform the function of creating those values:

> Within an ironist culture. . . it is the disciplines which specialize in thick description of the private and idiosyncratic which are assigned a job. In particular, novels and ethnographies which sensitize one to the pain of those who do not speak our language must do the job which demonstration of a common human nature was supposed to do.[11]

II

I am in agreement with a great deal of Rorty's analysis, especially with his pragmatism and with the account that he gives of what is happening in contemporary theory. I certainly subscribe to his rejection of any metaphysical grounding of the social order and with his critique of Habermas. Finally, I also endorse his defence of the liberal democratic framework. However, I think that there is in his 'liberal utopia' something which simply does not work. And I do not think that it is a matter of detail or incompletion but an internal inconsistency of his 'ideal society'.

Let us start with his characterization of liberal society as a type of social arrangement in which persuasion substitutes for force. My main difficulty is that I cannot establish between the two as sharp a distinction as Rorty does. Of course, in one sense the distinction *is* clear: in persuasion there is an element of consensus while in force there is not. But the question which remains is: to what extent in persuasion/consensus is there not an ingredient of force? What is it to persuade? Except in the extreme case of proving something to somebody in an algorithmic way, we are engaged in an operation which involves making somebody change her opinion without any ultimate rational foundation. Rorty quite correctly limits the domain of reason to the interior of any particular language game, but the difficulty subsists, because language games are not absolutely closed universes and, as a consequence, decisions within them have to be made which are undecidable by the system of rules which define the structure of the game. I agree with Rorty/Davidson that recognition of this fact does not justify describing the decision as irrational, and that the whole distinction between rational and irrational is of little use. But what I want to point out is something different: it is that a decision to be made under those conditions is going to inevitably include an element of force. Let us take Davidson's example of somebody who wants to reform herself and decides to suppress a desire – for example, an alcoholic who decides to stop drinking. From the point of view of the desire there is only repression – that is force. And this argument can be generalized. Let us consider various possible situations:

Situation A

I am confronted with the need to choose between several possible courses of action, and the structure of the language game that I am playing is indifferent to them. After having evaluated the situation, I conclude that there is no obvious candidate for my decision but I nevertheless make *one* choice. It is clear that in this case I have repressed the alternative courses of action.

Situation B

I want to persuade somebody to change his opinion. As the belief I want to inculcate in him is not the Hegelian truth of the opposed belief that he actually has, what I want to do is not to *develop* his belief but to *cancel it out* of existence. Again, force. Let us suppose that I succeed in my efforts. In that case, he has been *converted* to my belief. But the element of force is always there. All I have done is to convince my friend that he becomes my ally in killing his belief. Persuasion, consequently, structurally involves force.

Situation C

There are two possible courses of action and two groups of people are split about which to follow. As the two courses of action are equally possible within the structure of the situation, the *différend* can only be solved by force. Of course this element of force will be actualized in many different ways: either by one group persuading the other (and we are back to situation *B*); or through a system of rules accepted by both parts to settle the *différend* (a vote for instance); or by the *ultima ratio*. But the important point to see is that the element of force is going to be present in all cases.

Clearly the kind of society that Rorty prefers is that in which the third solution to situation C is excluded, but this still presents various difficulties. The first is that it is simply not possible to oppose force and persuasion given that persuasion is *one* form of force. The discussion is thus displaced to an analysis of the way in which force is organized in society and of the types of force that are acceptable in a liberal society. The second problem is that the element of physical force cannot be eliminated even in the freest of societies. I doubt that Rorty would advocate persuasion as an adequate method of dealing with a rapist. And strikes, or student sit-ins – which are perfectly legitimate actions in a free society – try to achieve their goals not only through persuasion but also by forcing their antagonist to surrender to violence. There are, of course, many intermediate cases.

For the same reasons I tend to deal with the distinction between reform and revolution in a different way from Rorty. In my view, the problem is to displace the terrain which made the distinction possible. For the classical ideal of Revolution does not involve only the dimension of violence that Rorty underlines but also the idea that this violence had to be directed towards a very specific end, which was to give a *new foundation* to the social order. Now, from this point of view I am a reformist, not because my social aims are limited but simply because I do not believe that society has such a thing as a foundation. No doubt Rorty would agree with me on this point. Even the events which in the past *have been called* revolutions were only the overdetermination of a multiplicity of reforms which cover vast aspects of society but by no means the totality of them. The idea of turning the whole society upside-down does not make any sense. (Which does not mean that many ugly things were not committed in the attempt to perform this impossible operation.) But if, on the one hand, I am trying to relocate revolution within reform, on the other hand, I am very much in favour of reintroducing the dimension of violence within reform. A world in which reform takes place without violence is not a world in which I would like to live. It could be either an absolutely unidimensional society, in which 100 per cent of the population would agree with any single reform, or one in which the decisions would be made by an army of social engineers with the backing of the rest of the population. Any reform involves changing the *status quo* and in most cases this will hurt existing interests. The process of reform is a process of struggles, not a process of quiet piecemeal engineering. And there is nothing here to regret. It is in this active process of struggle that human abilities – new language games – are created. Could we, for instance, think what the workers' identity would have been without the active struggles with which they were involved during the first stages of industrial societies? Certainly many of the workers' abilities which will be essential to the process of democratization of Western societies would not have developed. And the same, of course, can be said of any other social force. Thus, the radical democratic 'utopia' that I would like to counterpose to Rorty's liberal one does not preclude antagonisms and social division but, on the contrary, considers them as constitutive of the social.

So, in my view, Rorty has based his argument on certain types of polarization – persuasion/force, reform/violence-revolution – which are not only simplistic but also inconsistent because the role of the goodies presupposes the presence, inside it, of baddies. Any theory about power in a democratic society has to be a theory about the forms of power which are compatible with democracy, not about the elimination of power. And this is not the result of any particular persistence of a form of domination but of the very fact that society, as Rorty knows well, is not structured as a jigsaw puzzle and that, as a consequence, it is impossible to avoid the collision of different demands and language games with each other. Let us take the case of recent debates in America concerning pornography. Various feminist groups have argued that pornography offends women – something with which I could not agree more. But some of these groups have gone so far as to ask for legislation permitting any woman to take to court the publishers of the pornographic material or advertisement. This has raised the objection – which I also share – that this would create a climate of intimidation which could affect freedom of expression. Where should the line be drawn between what is pornographic and what is artistic expression, for instance?

Obviously a balance has to be established between antagonistic demands. But it is important to stress that the balance is not going to be the result of having found a point at which both demands harmonize with each other – in which case, we would be back to the jigsaw puzzle theory. No, the antagonism of the two demands is, in that context, ineradicable, and the balance consists of limiting the effects of both so that a sort of social equilibrium – something very different from a rational harmonization – can be reached. But, in that case, the antagonism, though socially regulated and controlled, will subsist under the form of what could be called a 'war of position'. Each pole of the conflict will have a certain power and will exercise a certain violence over the other pole. The paradoxical corollary of this conclusion is that the existence of violence and antagonisms is the very condition of a free society. The reason for this is that antagonism results from the fact that the social is not a plurality of effects radiating from a pre-given centre, but is pragmatically constructed from many starting points. But it is precisely because of this, because there is an ontological possibility of clashes and unevenness, that we can speak of freedom. Let us suppose that we move to the opposite hypothesis, the one contained in the classical notion of emancipation – that is a society from which violence and antagonisms have been *entirely* eliminated. In this society, we can only enjoy the Spinozian freedom of being conscious of necessity. This is a first paradox of a free community: that which constitutes its condition of impossibility (violence) constitutes at the same time its condition of possibility. Particular forms of oppression can be eliminated, but freedom only exists in so far as the achievement of a total freedom is an ever receding horizon. A totally free society and a totally determined society would be, as I have argued elsewhere, exactly the same. I think that the reason why Rorty is not entirely aware of these antinomies is the result of his insufficient theorization of what is involved in the notion of 'persuasion' and of the total opposition he has established between 'persuasion' and 'force'.

III

Persuasion is an essentially impure notion. One cannot persuade without persuasion's other – that is, force. One can speak of the force of persuasion but one would never say that one had been 'persuaded' of the correctness of the Pythagorean theorem. The latter is simply *shown*, without any need for persuasion. But one cannot say either that persuasion is simply *reducible* to force. Persuasion is the terrain of what Derrida would have called a 'hymen'. It is the point in which the 'reasons' for a belief and the 'causes' of the belief constitute an inseparable whole. The adoption of a new paradigm in Kuhnian terms is a good example of what I mean. A multitude of small reasons/causes ranging from theoretical difficulties to technical advances in the tools of scientific research overdetermine each other in determining the transition from normal to revolutionary science. And for reasons that I have explained earlier – and which are also clearly present in some way in Kuhn's account – this transition is not an indifferent and painless abandonment but involves repression of other possibilities, it is the result of a struggle. This is obviously more clearly visible when we refer to the politico-ideological field. Now, as I have argued with Chantal Mouffe in *Hegemony and Socialist Struggle*, there is a name in our political tradition which refers to this peculiar operation called persuasion which is only constituted through its inclusion, within itself, of its violent opposite: this name is 'hegemony'.

I refer to our book for all aspects concerning the genealogy of the concept of hegemony from the Russian social-democrats to Gramsci, for its structural characteristics and for its forms of theoretical articulation within the project of a radical democracy. Here I want only to underline some aspects which are relevant to the present discussion. The most important one is that 'hegemony' is the discursive terrain in which foundationalism began disintegrating in the history of Marxism. What had been so far presented as a necessary consequence of an endogenous development determined by the contradiction between development of the productive forces and existing relations of production, became, escalating from Lenin to Gramsci, the result of a contingent process of political articulation in an open ensemble whose elements had purely relational identities. That is that History (with a capital 'H') was not a valid object of discourse because it did not correspond to any a priori unified object. The only thing we had was the discontinuous succession of hegemonic blocs which was not governed by any rationally graspable logic – neither teleological, nor dialectical or causal. As in the relation between the desire that I want to suppress – in Davidson's example – and the decision to suppress it, there is no internal connection at all. On the other hand, there is an important dialectic here to detect between necessity and contingency. If each of the elements intervening in a hegemonic bloc had an identity of its own, its relations with all the others would be merely contingent; but if, on the contrary, the identity of all elements is contingent upon its relations with the others, those relations, *if* the identity is going to be maintained, are absolutely necessary.

Now, the problem to be discussed is the internal logic of the hegemonic operation which underlies the process of persuasion. We will approach it by bringing to the analysis various devices which are thinkable as a result of the transformations which have taken place in contemporary theory. Let us start with the Wittgensteinian example of the rule governing the sequence of a numerical series. I say 'one, two, three, four' and ask a friend to continue it: the spontaneous answer would be to say 'five, six, seven,' etcetera. But I can say that the series I have in mind is not that but 'one, two, three, four, nine, ten, eleven, twelve,' etcetera.

My friend thinks that he has now understood and proceeds accordingly, but I can still say that the series is not what I had in mind, etcetera. The rule governing the series can be indefinitely changed. Everything depends, as Lewis Carroll would put it, on who is in command. Let us slightly change the example now. Let us suppose that we are speaking of a game in which player *A* starts a series and player *B* has to continue it the way he wants, providing that there is some visible regularity. Now, when it is again *A*'s turn he has to invent a new rule which takes as its starting point the series as it has been left by *B* and so on. In the end, the loser is the one who finds the whole business so complicated that he is unable to imagine a new rule. The corollaries which follow from this example are the following: (a) that there is no such thing as the ultimate rule: it can always be subverted; (b) that as an indefinite number of players can come to participate in the game, the rule governing the series is essentially threatened – it is, to use Rorty's expression, *radically contingent*; (c) that the identity of each of the individual figures within the series is entirely relational, it is given only by its structural position within the rule that is at that moment hegemonizing the series, and it will change with the formulation of a new rule. I think this is important because the process of persuasion is frequently described as if somebody who has a belief *A* is presented with a belief *B* and the suggestion is of moving from one to the other. Things never happen that way. What happens is, rather, that new elements enter into the picture and the old rule is unable to hegemonize them – as if, for instance, an apparently chaotic series of numbers is introduced into our series and the challenge is to find a coherent rule which will be compatible with the new state of affairs. Very frequently the new rule is accepted, not because it is liked in itself, but just because it is a rule, because it introduces a principle of coherence and intelligibility in an apparent chaos. In the confused Italian situation of the early 1920s, many liberals accepted Fascism not because they particularly liked it, but because an explosive social situation existed which was both unthinkable and unmanageable within the framework of the traditional political system, and Fascism appeared the *only* coherent discourse which could deal with the new chaotic events. And if liberalism had wanted – which it did not – to present itself as an alternative hegemonic discourse articulating the new elements, it could only have done so by transforming itself. Between the liberalism of 1905 and the liberalism of 1922 there are only 'family resemblances'. This is because, among other reasons, the latter had to be anti-fascist and this involved dealing with a new series of problems that radically transformed the discursive field. This is the reason why I do not agree with Rorty's assertion that we can be *just* liberals; that our 'we' has reached a point which does not require any further transformation. Even if we want to continue being liberals we will always have to be something more. Liberalism can only exist as a hegemonic attempt in this process of articulation – as a result of the radically relational character of all identity. Here I think that Rorty has not been historicist enough.

This is also the point – moving from Wittgenstein to Derrida – at which deconstruction becomes central for a theory of politics. Derrida has shown the essential vulnerability of all context. In his words:

> Every sign, linguistic or not linguistic, spoken or written (in the current sense of this opposition), in a small or large unit, can be *cited*, put between quotation marks; in so doing it can break with every given context, engendering an infinitude of new contexts in a manner which is absolutely illimitable. This does not imply that the mark is valid outside of a context, but on the contrary that there are only contexts without any centre of absolute anchorage (*anchrage*). This citationality, this duplication or duplicity, this iterability of the mark is neither an accident nor an anomaly, it is that (normal/abnormal) without which a mark could not even have a function called 'normal'. What would a mark be that could not be cited? Or one whose origins would not get lost along the way?[12]

Now, what is this saying if not that all context is essentially vulnerable and open, that the fact that one of the possibilities rather than the others has been chosen is a purely *contingent* fact? If the choice is not *determined* by the structure, it is down to the bottom a hegemonic operation, an essentially *political* decision.

Let us go back, with this distinction in mind, to Rorty's text. The first aspect of his liberal utopia with which I would take issue is his sharp division between the public and the private. It is not, of course, that I want to return to some 'grand theory' which would embrace both. The reason for my disagreement is exactly the opposite: Rorty sees as necessarily united many things which, for me, are radically discontinuous and held together only through contingent articulations. Is the realm of personal self-realization really a *private* realm? It would be so if that self-realization took place in a neutral medium in which individuals could seek unimpeded the fulfilment of their own aims. But this medium is, of course, a myth. A woman searching for her self-realization will find obstacles in the form of male oriented rules which will limit her *personal* aspirations and possibilities. The feminist struggles tending to change those rules will constitute a collective 'we' *different* from the 'we' of abstract public citizenship, but the space which these struggles create – remember the motto 'the personal is political' – will be no less a communitarian and public space than the one in which political parties intervene and in which elections are fought. And the same can be said, of course, of any struggle which begins as a result of the existence of social norms, prejudices, regulations, etcetera that frustrate the self-realization of an individual. I see the *strength* of the democratic society in the multiplication of these public spaces and its *condition* in the recognition of their plurality and autonomy. This recognition is based on the essential *discontinuity* existing between those social spaces, and the essential character of these discontinuities makes possible its exact opposite: the contingent-hegemonic articulation among them of what could be called a global sense of community, a certain democratic common sense. We see here a second paradox of community: it has to be essentially unachievable to become pragmatically possible. So, what about the private? It is a residual category, limited to those aspects of our activity in which our objectives are not interfered with by any structural social barrier, in which their achievement does not require the constitution of any struggling community, of any 'we'. So, as we see, the classical terms of the problem are displaced: it is no longer a question of preventing a public space from encroaching upon that of private individuals, given that the public spaces have to be constituted in order to achieve individual aims. But the condition for a democratic society is that these public spaces have to be plural: a democratic society is, of course, incompatible with the existence of only *one* public space. What we should have is a multiple 'civic republicanism'.

As is clear, my idea of a democratic society is different in central respects from Rorty's liberal utopia. Rorty's utopia consists of a public space limited – as for all good liberals – to minimal functions and a private sphere in which individual agents seek their own ends. This system can certainly be reformed and improved, but one has the impression that such improvements are of the type of improving a machine by designing a better model, not the result of struggles. Antagonism and violence do not play either a positive or negative role, simply because they are entirely absent from the picture. For me, a radically democratic society is one in which a plurality of public spaces, constituted around specific issues and demands, and strictly autonomous of each other, instils in its members a civic sense which is a central ingredient of their identity as individuals. Despite the plurality of these spaces, or, rather, as a consequence of it, a diffuse democratic culture is created, which gives the community its specific identity. Within this community, the liberal institutions – parliament, elections, divisions of power – are maintained, but these are one public space, not *the* public space. Not only is antagonism not excluded from a democratic society, it is the very condition of its institution.

For Rorty the three words 'bourgeois liberal democracy' constitute an indivisible whole; for me there is between them only a contingent articulation. As a socialist I am prepared to fight against capitalism for the hegemony of liberal institutions and, as a believer in the latter, I am prepared to do my best to make them compatible with the whole field of democratic public spaces, but I see this compatibility as a hegemonic construction, not as something granted from the beginning. I think that a great deal of twentieth-century history can be explained by dislocations in the articulation of the three components just mentioned. Liberal institutions (let alone capitalism) have fared badly in Third World countries and of the attempt to articulate socialism and democracy (if attempt it can be called) in the countries of the Eastern bloc, the record is simply appalling. Though my preference is for a liberal-democratic-socialist society, it is clear to me that if I am forced under given circumstances to choose one out of the three, my preference will always be for democracy. (For instance, if in a Third World country I have to choose between, on the one hand, a corrupt and repressive liberal regime, in which elections are a farce manipulated by clientelistic gangs, with no participation of the masses; and on the other, a nationalist military regime which tends to social reform and the self-organization of the masses, my preference will be for the latter. All my experience shows that, while in some cases the second type of regime can lead – with many difficulties – to an increasing liberalization of its institutions, the opposite process does not take place in the first case: it is just a blind alley.)

IV

Finally, I want to address the two possible objections to the argument that Rorty raises (see above), and his answers to them. Regarding the first objection, I think that Rorty is entirely correct and I have nothing to add. But in the case of the second objection, I feel that Rorty's answer is unnecessarily defensive and that a much better argument can be made. I would formulate it this way. The question is whether the abandonment of universalism undermines the foundation of a democratic society. My answer is yes, I grant the whole argument. Without a universalism of sorts – the idea of human rights, for instance – a truly democratic society is impossible. But in order to assert this, it is not at all necessary to muddle through the Enlightenment's rationalism or Habermas's 'domination-free communication'. It is enough to recognize that democracy needs universalism while asserting, at the same time, that universalism is one of the vocabularies, of the language games, which was constructed at some point by social agents and it has become a more and more central part of our values and our culture. It is a *contingent* historical product. It originated in religious discourse – all men are equal before God – was brought down to this world by the Enlightenment, and has been generalized to wider and wider social relations by the democratic revolution of the last two centuries.

A historicist recasting of universalism has, I would think, two main political advantages over its metaphysical version, and these, far from weakening it, help to reinforce and to radicalize it. The first is that it has a liberating effect: human beings will begin seeing themselves more and more as the exclusive authors of their world. The historicity of being will become more apparent. If people think that God or nature have made the world as it is, they will tend to consider their fate inevitable. But if the being of the world which they inhabit is only the result of the contingent discourses and vocabularies that constitute it, they will tolerate their fate with less patience and will stand a better chance of becoming political 'strong poets'. The second advantage is that the perception of the contingent character of universalist values will make us all more conscious of the dangers which threaten them and of their possible extinction. If we happen to believe in those values, the consciousness of their historicity will not make us more indifferent to them but, on the contrary, will make us more responsible citizens, more ready to engage in their defence. Historicism, in this way, helps those who believe in those values. As for those who do not believe in them, no rationalist argument will ever have the slightest effect.

This leads me to a last point. This double effect – increasing freeing of human beings through a more assertive image of their capacities, increasing social responsibility through the conscience of the historicity of being – is the most important possibility, a radically political possibility, that contemporary thought is opening to us. The metaphysical discourse of the West is coming to an end, and philosophy in its twilight has performed, through the great names of the century, a last service for us: the deconstruction of its own terrain and the creation of the conditions for its own impossibility. Let us think, for instance, of Derrida's undecidables. Once undecidability has reached the ground itself, once the organization of a certain camp is governed by a hegemonic decision – hegemonic because it is not objectively determined, because different decisions were also possible – the realm of philosophy comes to an end and the realm of politics begins. This realm will be inhabited by a different type of discourse, by discourses such as Rorty's 'narratives', which tend to construct the world on the grounds of a radical undecidability. But I do not like the name 'ironist' – which evokes all kinds of playful images – for this political strong poet. On the contrary, someone who is confronted with Auschwitz and has the moral strength to admit the contingency of her own beliefs, instead of seeking refuge in religious or rationalistic myths is, I think, a profoundly heroic and tragic figure. This will be a hero of a new type who has still not been entirely created by our culture, but one whose creation is absolutely necessary if our time is going to live up to its most radical and exhilarating possibilities.

Notes

1. Ernesto Laclau and Chantal Mouffe, *Hegemony and Socialist Strategy: Towards a Radical Democratic Politics*, London, Verso 1985.
2. Richard Rorty, *Contingency, Irony and Solidarity,* Cambridge, Cambridge University Press 1989, p. xv.
3. Ibid. p. 9.
4. Ibid. p. 29.
5. Ibid. p. 30.
6. Ibid. p. 35.
7. Ibid. p. 46.
8. Ibid.
9. Ibid. pp. 51–2.
10. Ibid. pp. 60–1.
11. Ibid. p. 94.
12. Jacques Derrida, 'Signature Event Context', in *Limited Inc.*, Evanston, Northwestern University Press 1988, p. 12.

Index

Phronesis titles from Verso

MICHEL FOUCAULT
Genealogy as Critique
Rudi Visker
Translated by Chris Turner

FOR THEY KNOW NOT WHAT THEY DO
Enjoyment as a Political Factor
Slavoj Žižek

THE SUBLIME OBJECT OF IDEOLOGY
Slavoj Žižek

Printed in the United States
by Baker & Taylor Publisher Services